ILLUSTRATED ENCYCLOPEDIA

HOUSEPLANT
IDENTIFIER

ILLUSTRATED ENCYCLOPEDIA

HOUSEPLANT
IDENTIFIER

PETER MCHOY

SELECT
EDITIONS

Select Editions imprint specially produced
for Selectabook Ltd

Produced by Anness Publishing Limited
Hermes House, 88-89 Blackfriars Road,
London SE1 8HA

A CIP catalogue record for this book is
available from the British Library

ISBN 1 84038 820 X

Publisher: Joanna Lorenz
Senior Editor: Clare Nicholson
Designer: Peter Butler
Photographer: John Freeman

Production Controller: Don Campaniello

Previously published as *The New Houseplant A-Z*,
and as part of a larger compendium, *The Complete
Guide to Houseplants*

Printed and bound in China

ACKNOWLEDGEMENTS
The publishers would like to thank the following for
their generous help in the production of this book:
Andrew J Smith, Manor Nuseries, Stockbridge Road,
Timsbury, Hants; Chessington Nurseries Ltd, Leatherhead Road,
Chessington, Surrey; and The Hollygate Cactus Nursery,
Billingshurst Lane, Ashington, West Sussex.

All photography by John Freeman, with additional photographs,
as follows:

Key: t = top; b = bottom; l = left; r = right; c = centre

Peter McHoy: pages 19, 20 bl, 23 t, 27, 32 b, 38 t, 50 br, 53 bl cl,
62, 63 b, 66 tc, 71tr br, 83 b, 85 t, 102 b, 108 bl, 115 and 125 t b;
The Garden Picture Library: pages 6 (Erika Craddock), 80 t (John Sira),
112 (Mayer Lescanff), 124 br (John Sira); A-Z Botanical: pages 82 l;
and photos Horticultural: pages 68 t, 93 bl and 111b.

Contents

Introduction

Most of the houseplants in the following pages can be found in garden centres and shops, and the many illustrations will allow you to use the book for identification as well as for practical advice. No book can be totally comprehensive, of course, and if you begin to collect particular groups of plants such as bromeliads, cacti or orchids, you will find many more varieties at specialist nurseries. In most cases, these varieties are likely to prefer similar conditions and care to those mentioned in this book.

Finding the right name

Sometimes botanists change the names of old favourites, and it is not un-known for other botanists to change them again – even back to the original name! Sometimes new names are taken up quickly, but often it is many years, even decades, before a new name be-comes accepted by nurserymen and gardeners.

In this book the up-to-date names are mentioned to make the book as complete as possible, but the entry is likely to be found under the name by which the plant is commonly sold. Wherever applicable the names have been cross-referenced, so you should be able to find the plant whether you normally use the 'old' or 'new' name.

In common with many books, we have used the word 'variety' in its colloquial sense, rather than the more botanically correct 'cultivar', 'variety' or 'varietas', and 'forma', which makes for difficult reading and is of no practical value to the gardener. The typographical presentation of the names is, however, correct.

If you know a plant only by its common name, look it up in the common name index. This will give you the Latin name under which you will find the entry.

OPPOSITE: *A selection of houseplants*

Reading the entries

Genus This is equivalent to a sur-name, identifying the group of plants with common characteristics.

Species This is equivalent to a fore-name, identifying an individual plant within the genus. Sometimes there is only one species in a genus, but usual-ly there are many – sometimes hun-dreds. Those listed are the species you are most likely to encounter when buying houseplants.

Temperature Except where a plant is frost-sensitive (when it is very impor-tant to prevent the plant freezing), the temperatures given are target minima. But the majority of plants will not come to any harm if the temperature drops lower – they may not thrive or grow as well, but they are unlikely to die. Maximum temperatures are not given, as in most households it is not practical to reduce the summer air temperature signifi-cantly. When a high winter tempera-ture caused by central heating may be detrimental – perhaps shortening the flowering period – a suggested max-imum has been given.

Humidity The amount of moisture in the air can be crucial. Plants from tropical rain forests may demand very moist or humid air, yet desert plants will often tolerate air drier than you are likely to find in the home. Avoid those that require high humidity un-less you can provide it . . . or are

ABOVE: Columnea gloriosa

prepared to treat the plant simply as a short-term decoration for the home.

Position This can be crucial – if the light is bad many plants grow poorly and fail to thrive. Other plants will be scorched (develop brown burn marks on the leaves) or even die if placed in a hot and sunny spot.

Watering and feeding Never water by the calendar alone, and always use your own discretion when deciding whether a plant requires more water. This book indicates periods of high or low water needs. Feeding should nev-er be neglected, but the advice here is based on periods of need rather than frequency of feeding. Frequency de-pends on the type of fertilizer being used – follow the instructions on the fertilizer label.

Care Useful hints and tips that will help you get the best from your plant.

Propagation Detailed propagation techniques are beyond the scope of this book, but the main methods used are given for guidance. If sowing seed, follow the information on the packet or in the catalogue. Cuttings are likely to require a heated propaga-tor during cold months, but should root at air temperature during the summer. The best type of cutting may depend on the time of year it is taken, so consult a propagation book for the trickier subjects if in doubt.

ABOVE: Achimenes *hybrid*

Achimenes

True species are sometimes grown, but the plants you are most likely to find are hybrids. Specialist nurseries offer a large range of named varieties, and the rhizomes are often sold by bulb merchants and seedsmen.

Achimenes hybrids

The short-lived flowers, in shades of pink, purple, yellow, red, and white, are produced in abundance from early summer to autumn. The plants die down in winter but grow again the following spring.

HELPFUL HINTS

Temperature Undemanding as the plant dies down for the winter. Aim for a minimum 13°C (55°F) while growing.
Humidity Mist frequently when the flower buds are developing, then provide humidity without spraying by standing the pot on a tray of pebbles.
Position Good light, but avoid exposing to direct sun.
Watering and feeding Water with tepid, soft water during the growing season. Never allow the compost (potting soil) to dry out. Feed regularly.
Care Grow in a hanging pot if you want its weak stems to cascade, otherwise support them with thin canes. Stop watering when the plant begins to drop its leaves in autumn. Leave the rhizomes in the pot or remove and store in peat (moss peat) or sand in a frost-free place. Start into growth or replant in late winter or early spring.
Propagation Division of rhizomes; cuttings; seed (not named varieties).

Adiantum

These delicate-looking ferns include a few species that are frost-tolerant, but most are delicate plants that need warmth and high humidity and they can be difficult to keep for long in a living-room. The small ones do well in a bottle garden.

Adiantum capillus-veneris

Thin, feathery-looking fronds on dark stems. This fern is the toughest of those described. In some countries this is known commercially as *A. chilense*, though there is a distinct plant with this name.

Adiantum chilense *see A. capillus-veneris*.

Adiantum cuneatum *see A. raddianum*.

Adiantum hispidulum

A coarser-looking fern than most adiantums, although the new fronds are a delicate pinkish-bronze.

BELOW: Adiantum hispidulum

ABOVE: Adiantum raddianum *'Fragrantissimum', also known as 'Fragrans' (left), and 'Fritz Luthii' (right)*
LEFT: Adiantum capillus-veneris

Care Most problems arise from dry or cool air. Never let the compost (potting soil) dry out, but do not leave the pot standing in water.
Propagation Division is the easiest method, but spores can be sown in spring.

Adiantum raddianum
One of the most popular species, with erect young fronds that later curve. If conditions suit, it will make a medium-sized pot plant. There are many varieties, with slight variations in leaf shape or colour and growth habit. 'Fragrantissimum' is slightly aromatic. 'Fritz-Luthii' has bright green fronds. Also known as *A. cuneatum.*

HELPFUL HINTS
Temperature A winter minimum of 18°C (64°F) is generally advisable for most species.
Humidity High humidity is essential for good results.
Position Shaded from direct sun and away from cold draughts.
Watering and feeding Water freely throughout the year. Apply a weak fertilizer from spring to early autumn.

Aechmea

The most widely grown species, *A. fasciata,* is one of the best-known of the bromeliads, with attractive foliage and a spectacular and long-lasting flower head.

Aechmea fasciata
Large green leaves, banded silvery-grey, form an urn-like rosette. The spiky-looking flower head has pink bracts and small blue flowers that fade to lilac. The main flowering season is mid summer to early winter; individual heads can remain attractive for months, but the rosette dies afterwards. The plant is sometimes seen under its old name of *A. rhodocyanea.*

Aechmea rhodocyanea *see A. fasciata.*

HELPFUL HINTS
Temperature Winter minimum 15°C (59°F), unless you intend to discard the plant after flowering.
Humidity Undemanding.
Position Good light, but avoid exposing to direct sun.
Watering and feeding Keep roots moist at all times, top up water in funnel in summer, but empty it in winter unless the temperature is above 18°C (64°F). Feed with a weak fertilizer in summer.
Care Young plants raised at home will not flower for several years, but to stimulate flowering on a mature plant, enclose in a plastic bag with a couple of ripe apples for a few days. The gasses released may induce flowering. Mist only on hot days. After flowering, that part of the plant will die, but offsets will be produced that can be used for propagation.
Propagation Remove the young rosettes when about half the height of the parent. Pot up, retaining as much of the root system as possible.

BELOW: Aechmea fasciata

Aeschynanthus

Several species may be grown as houseplants, but the one described is among the most successful. Even this is better in a conservatory than a living-room. All have trailing stems with leathery leaves and clusters of red or orange flowers.

Aeschynanthus lobbianus

Dark green, fleshy leaves on trailing stems, with terminal clusters of bright flowers with brownish-purple calyces and red flowers lightly flushed with yellow. Flowering time is usually early summer.

HELPFUL HINTS

Temperature Warm in summer, cool in winter, but with a minimum of 13°C (55°F).
Humidity Mist frequently all year round, especially in hot weather.
Position Good light, but not direct sun.
Watering and feeding Water freely from spring to autumn, sparingly at other times. Use soft, tepid water if possible. Feed in summer.

Care After flowering, shorten the stems to prevent the plant becoming too straggly. Moving a plant in flower to a different position may sometimes cause the blooms to drop. It is a good

ABOVE: Aeschynanthus *hybrid 'Mona'*

idea to repot the plants every second or third year.
Propagation Cuttings.

Agave

Although often regarded as succulents, agaves are xerophytes (plants able to survive in areas with scanty water supplies). Some have magnificent flower spikes where they are able to grow outdoors, but they are regarded as foliage plants indoors. *A. americana* is often used in a tub as a patio plant, and in mild areas can sometimes be overwintered successfully outdoors.

Agave americana

Large grey-green or blue-grey, strap-like leaves, often 1–1.2m (3–4ft) long in favourable conditions, and with sharp spines. As a pot plant it is

LEFT: Agave americana
OPPOSITE TOP: Agave victoriae-reginae

usually grown in one of its variegated forms such as 'Marginata', 'Mediopicta' or 'Variegata'.

Agave filifera

A rounded rosette of stiff, fleshy, pointed leaves that curve upwards, with thread-like growths.

Agave victoriae-reginae

Dull-green, white-edged triangular leaves, forming an almost spherical rosette. One of the best agaves as a houseplant.

HELPFUL HINTS

Temperature Winter minimum 10°C (50°F) is adequate for all species. Some will tolerate lower temperatures but keep frost-free.

Humidity Tolerates dry air.

Position Full sun.

Watering and feeding Water as required in summer, but keep almost dry in winter (water occasionally if the light is good). Feed occasionally during the summer.

Care Stand large plants such as *A. americana* outdoors for the summer (but beware of any spines if placing on a patio). Repot each spring.

Propagation Root the runners or separate the young plants that form around the bases of some species. Can be raised from seed, but growth tends to be slow.

Aglaonema

Clump-forming plants with spear-shaped leaves on short stems arising from the base. The plain green ones lack interest, but the variegated species and varieties make attractive and tolerant houseplants.

Aglaonema crispum

Green leaves with silvery-grey patches. 'Marie' has particularly good variegation.

Aglaonema commutatum

Green leaves crossed with silvery bands. Inconspicuous greenish-white flowers are sometimes followed by red berries.

Aglaonema hybrids

Some of the best aglaonemas to use as houseplants are hybrids. 'Silver Queen' has silver and green leaves, 'Silver King' has leaves almost entirely silvery-grey and spotted leaf stalks.

The nomenclature of aglaonemas has been confused, and you will sometimes find these listed as varieties of *A. treubii*.

HELPFUL HINTS

Temperature Aim for a winter minimum of 15°C (59°F), although plants will continue to grow at 10°C (50°F).

Humidity Needs high humidity. Mist regularly.

Position All-green aglaonemas tolerate low light levels, but variegated forms need only light shade. Avoid direct sun.

Watering and feeding Water freely spring to autumn, sparingly in winter. Feed from spring to autumn.

Care Best in shallow pots. The plants are slow-growing so repot only when necessary.

Propagation Cuttings. Division.

BELOW LEFT: Aglaonema crispum *'Marie'*

Aloe

Aloes are trouble-free succulents with a dramatic appearance, which makes them useful as specimen houseplants for a sunny windowsill.

Aloe arborescens
Erect growth with tentacle-like fleshy leaves, edged with sharp thorns. May produce spikes of attractive orange-red flowers. Will make a tall plant in time, but growth is relatively slow if restricted in a pot.

Aloe ferox
Thick, fleshy leaves with reddish-brown spines over the surface that give the plant a warty appearance. Mature plants produce branching red flower spikes. Grows to about 45cm (1½ft).

Aloe mitriformis
Fleshy blue-green leaves, conspicuously spined around the edge and on the back. Dull scarlet flowers in summer.

Aloe variegata
Forms a rosette of triangular, dark green, purple-tinged leaves with V-shaped white bands. Red flowers are sometimes produced. Makes a compact plant that grows to about 15–30cm (6–12in) tall.

HELPFUL HINTS
Temperature Cool but frost-free in winter. Aim for about 5°C (41°F).
Humidity Tolerates dry air.
Position Full sun. Can stand in the garden in summer.
Watering and feeding Water a couple of times a week in summer, sparingly in winter. Feed occasionally in summer.
Routine care Repot in spring every second or third year.
Propagation Offsets (sever carefully with as much root system as possible). Seed in spring.

LEFT: Aloe ferox
BELOW: Aloe variegata

Ananas

The ornamental pineapples grown as houseplants sometimes have small inedible fruits. These are an interesting bonus, but ananas are grown primarily as foliage plants indoors.

Ananas bracteatus striatus
Brightly striped, spiky leaves in green, cream and pink. Although this plant is often found under this name, you may also see it as the more correct *A. b. tricolor*.

Ananas comosus variegatus
This is a variegated form of the edible pineapple. The plain green species is an unattractive houseplant, but this variegated form with lengthwise cream banding is more compact and appealing.

HELPFUL HINTS
Temperature Aim for 15–18°C (59–64°F) in winter.

Anthurium

Some species, such as *A. crystallinum* and *A. magnificum*, are grown as foliage plants, but the ones you are most likely to find are sold as flowering plants. They are difficult to keep indoors, but their distinctive flowers make them popular where a dramatic effect is required.

Anthurium andreanum
The plants sold under this name are almost always hybrids. One may also find the name with its more correct spelling of *A. andaeanum*. Heart-shaped leaves are produced on long stalks. The flowers have a large, shiny, red, pink, or white spathe and generally a straight spadix. Flowering is between spring and later summer, and the blooms last for several weeks.

Anthurium scherzerianum
The plants sold under this name are almost always hybrids. The leaves are

Humidity Undemanding, but mist in very hot weather.

Position Good light. The variegation is often better in sun. If placing on a windowsill, beware of the spines, which tend to catch on net curtains.

Watering and feeding Water freely in summer, cautiously in winter, and allow the soil to dry out a little before watering. Feed from late spring to early autumn.

Care In summer, occasionally add a little water to the vase formed by the rosette of leaves. Mature plants can be encouraged to flower by placing them in a plastic bag together with a few ripe apples or bananas for a few days.

Propagation Commercially, plants are often raised from seed, but for just a few plants it is quicker to use the crown of leaves on top of the fruit.

RIGHT: Ananas bracteatus striatus

lance- rather than heart-shaped and the spadix is curled. Flowering time for these plants is the same as for the previous species.

HELPFUL HINTS

Temperature Winter minimum 16°C (60°F).

Humidity Needs high humidity. Mist frequently, but avoid spraying the flowers.

Position Good light, but avoid exposing to direct summer sun.

Watering and feeding Water freely in summer, sparingly in winter. If possible use soft water. Feed with a weak fertilizer during summer.

Care Repot every second year, in spring, using a fibrous compost (potting mixture), and avoid over-firming.

Propagation Division. Stem cuttings and seeds are possible methods, but much more difficult.

LEFT: Anthurium scherzerianum

Aphelandra

The only species widely grown is a useful dual-purpose plant with attractive foliage and flowers.

Aphelandra squarrosa

Large, glossy, dark green leaves striped white along the veins. Conspicuous flower spike with long-lasting yellow bracts surrounding shorter-lived yellow flowers. The bracts overlap, giving a tiled effect, and remain attractive for a month or more. Flowering is usually in the autumn, but plants may bloom from late spring onwards and are sometimes available in flower in winter. The true species is not usually grown, and you are most likely to find more compact varieties such as 'Dania' and 'Louisae'.

HELPFUL HINTS

Temperature Winter minimum 13°C (55°F).

Humidity Needs high humidity. Mist frequently.

Position Good light; not direct sun. Good light induces flowering.

Watering and feeding Water freely in summer, less often in winter, but never let the compost become dry. Use soft water if possible. Feed regularly from spring to autumn.

Care Deadhead when flowering has finished. To prevent the leaves falling keep warm and humid, and away from cold draughts.

Propagation Stem cuttings in a propagator, in spring. Stem sections with a single eye can also be used.

BELOW: Aphelandra squarrosa

Aporocactus

A small group of undemanding cacti, the species described here being the ones most usually found. Of these, *A. flagelliformis* is most common. Although these trailing plants can be grafted on a taller rootstock, they are usually grown on their own roots and cascade over the edge of the pot.

Aporocactus flagelliformis

Circular trailing stems, with sharp spines. The red or pink flowers, large in relation to the size of the plant, are produced in spring.

Aporocactus flagriformis

Stronger and thornier stems than the previous species (although this is not always regarded as a distinct species).

Flowers are yellowish-red in bud and scarlet edged with violet when open.

HELPFUL HINTS

Temperature Winter minimum 5°C (41°F).
Humidity Tolerates dry air, but mist in very hot weather.
Position Full sun, but avoid intense afternoon sun. The plant can stand in the garden for the summer.
Watering and feeding Water freely in spring and summer, sparingly at other times.
Care Never move the plant once the buds have started to form, as this often causes them to drop. Keep in a cool, well-lit position in winter.
Propagation Cuttings; seed.

Araucaria

The species described is the only one normally grown as a pot plant, and is one of the few conifers used indoors. It makes a very large tree in the wild, but indoors grows into a majestic specimen plant of about 1.5m (5ft) after a few years. It needs space to grow symmetrically.

Araucaria excelsa *see A. heterophylla.*

Araucaria heterophylla
Tiers of stiff branches covered with prickly conifer needles about 1.5cm (⅝in) long. It is still sometimes sold under its old name of *A. excelsa.*

HELPFUL HINTS

Temperature Aim for 5–10°C (41–50°F) in winter.

Humidity Needs high humidity. Does not do well in a dry, centrally-heated room without regular misting.
Position Good light; not direct sun. Stand plant in the garden in summer.
Watering and feeding Water freely from spring to autumn, sparingly in winter. Never let the soil dry out. Use soft water if possible. Feed with a weak fertilizer in summer.
Care Try to avoid a hot room in winter. Repot only every third or fourth year to prevent the plant becoming too large.
Propagation Tip cuttings in a propagator, but amateurs usually have a low success rate.

BELOW: Araucaria heterophylla

Asparagus

Although popularly called ferns, these useful houseplants belong to the lily family and are not true ferns at all. The feathery-looking foliage, reduced to needle-like scales in many species, gives some of them a ferny appearance and they are a useful choice for a position that demands a tougher plant than most ferns. The species below are the most common, but others are sometimes available.

Asparagus densiflorus
The 'leaves' (technically cladophylls and not true leaves) are a fresh green and larger than those of A. setaceus, creating a more striking plant. The thread-like stems arch and become more pendulous as the plant grows older. Small white or pink flowers are sometimes produced and may be followed by red berries. The variety usually grown is 'Sprengeri'. 'Meyeri', sometimes listed as a separate species and more correctly spelt 'Myersii', is more erect and compact in habit.

Asparagus meyeri see A. densiflorus 'Meyeri' (syn. 'Myersii').

Asparagus plumosus see A. setaceus.

ABOVE: Asparagus densiflorus *'Sprengeri'* (syn. A. sprengeri)

Asparagus setaceus
Thread-like pale green 'leaves' (phyllodes) produce a feathery and ferny effect. Young plants are compact, but as they mature, long climbing shoots are produced. The plant is still widely known as A. *plumosus*.

Asparagus sprengeri see A. densiflorus 'Sprengeri'.

HELPFUL HINTS
Temperature Winter minimum 7°C (45°F). A. setaceus is best kept at a minimum 13°C (55°F).
Humidity Mist occasionally, especially in a centrally-heated room in winter. Mist A. setaceus in winter.
Position Good light or partial shade, but avoid exposing to direct sun.
Watering and feeding Water from spring to autumn, sparingly in winter. Feed from spring to early autumn.
Care Cut back by half a plant that has started to turn yellow or grown too large: it will often produce new shoots from lower down. Repot young plants every spring, older ones every second year.
Propagation Division; seed.

Aspidistra

Evergreen herbaceous plants with leaves that grow directly from soil level. The one species grown as a houseplant was once very popular because of its tough constitution and tolerance of poor growing conditions.

Aspidistra elatior
Large, dark green leaves about 45–60cm (1½-2ft) long, arising from the base. 'Variegata' has irregular creamy-white longitudinal stripes. Small purplish flowers sometimes appear at soil level in late winter or early spring, but usually go unnoticed.

HELPFUL HINTS
Temperature Keep cool but frost-free in winter, 7–10°C (45–50°F) is ideal.
Humidity Tolerates dry air.
Position Light or shade, but avoid exposing to direct sun.
Watering and feeding Water moderately from spring to autumn, sparingly in winter. Avoid waterlogging.
Care Wash or sponge the leaves occasionally to remove dust and improve light penetration. Repot only when really necessary – usually every four years or so.
Propagation Division.

BELOW: Aspidistra elatior

Asplenium

Of the many hundreds of species of this fern, including some that are hardy, only a few are regularly grown as houseplants. *Asplenium nidus* is especially popular because its thick, leathery leaves make it a much more tolerant houseplant than ferns with thinner and more delicate foliage.

Asplenium bulbiferum

Typical fern fronds, usually about 45–60cm (1½-2ft) tall. Small plantlets develop on the upper surfaces of mature leaves, which can be potted up to provide new plants.

Asplenium nidus

An epiphytic fern with glossy, undivided leaves that form a vase-like rosette. Mature plants may have brown spore cases on the undersides of the leaves.

HELPFUL HINTS

Temperature Winter minimum 13°C (55°F) for *A. bulbiferum,* 16°C (60°F) for *A. nidus.*
Humidity High humidity is essential.

ABOVE: Asplenium bulbiferum

Position Light or shade, but avoid exposing to direct sun.
Watering and feeding Water freely from spring to autumn, moderately in winter. Use soft water whenever possible.

Care Dust *A. nidus* leaves periodically. If brown or disfigured edges form on the leaves of *A. nidus*, these can often be successfully trimmed off with scissors — but avoid cutting into the green area.
Propagation Spores (difficult) or division. Pot up the plantlets of *A. bulbiferum.*

Aucuba

Frost-hardy shrubs widely planted in gardens, and often used as a houseplant for difficult situations where more tender plants would not thrive. You can plant them out in the garden if they grow too large, but acclimatize them first.

Aucuba japonica

Large, dark green, leathery leaves, blotched or spotted yellow in the varieties usually used as houseplants. There are many varieties, differing mainly in the amount of variegation. Popular ones, though often not identified on the label, are 'Crotonifolia' (boldly spotted and blotched gold), and 'Variegata' (speckled yellow). The inconspicuous flowers and red berries are seldom produced on indoor plants.

Although a large shrub of 1.5–1.8m (5–6ft) in the garden, it seldom grows to more than half this height when grown indoors in a pot.

HELPFUL HINTS

Temperature Undemanding and tolerates frost. Avoid high winter temperatures.
Humidity Tolerates dry air, but mist regularly in a warm room in winter.
Position Useful for shade but will grow in a light position. Avoid direct summer sun.
Watering and feeding Water freely spring to autumn, sparingly in winter.
Care Repot every second spring. Prune any over-long or sparse shoots at the same time.
Propagation Cuttings.

RIGHT: Aucuba japonica *variety*

Azalea

See *Rhododendron.*

Begonia – Foliage

Foliage begonias are attractive all year round. Although most foliage begonias will flower, the blooms are generally inconspicuous.

Begonia bowerae
Compact growth to about 15–23cm (6–9in), with small, bright green, brown-edged leaves, which are slightly serrated and hairy. Grows from a creeping rhizome. Single white flowers, tinged pink, in winter. Attractive hybrids include 'Tiger', heavily blotched bronze and green. Also spelled *B. boweri*.

Begonia listada
Lobed, dark green, softly hairy leaves with bright emerald green markings. A few white flowers in autumn and winter.

Begonia masoniana
Very distinctive, large, bright green, puckered leaves with a central brownish 'cross'. The flowers are insignificant.

Begonia rex
It is the hybrids of this important species that are now widely grown. There are named varieties, but the plants are usually sold as mixtures or unnamed. The asymmetrical leaves are about 23cm (9in) long and brightly variegated in shades of green, silver, brown, red, pink, and purple.

HELPFUL HINTS
Temperature Winter minimum 16°C (60°F).

Humidity Provide high humidity, but avoid spraying water directly onto the leaves.
Position Good light, but not direct sun.
Watering and feeding Water freely from spring to autumn, sparingly in winter.
Care Repot annually in spring.
Propagation Division; leaf cuttings.

Begonia – Flowering

Many begonias are grown for the beauty of their flowers – some for the prolific mass of small flowers over a long period (such as *B. semperflorens*, a very popular choice for a summer display in the garden); others, such as some of the tuberous hybrids, are grown for their less numerous, but larger, blooms.

Begonia × cheimantha *see B. lorraine hybrids.*

Begonia elatior hybrids
Single or double flowers in a wide colour range mainly in shades of red, pink, yellow, orange, and white. They are derived from crosses between *B. socotrana* and tuberous species from South America. The Rieger begonias belong to this group of hybrids, and these varieties are generally superior because they are less prone to mildew and bud-drop. The natural flowering period is winter, but commercial growers induce them to flower at all seasons. There are many named varieties.

This group of begonias is also known as *B. × hiemalis.*

Begonia × hiemalis *see B. elatior hybrids.*

Begonia lorraine hybrids
A cross between *B. socotrana* and *B. dregei*, and now botanically described as *B. × cheimantha,* this winter-flowering begonia has clusters of small pink or white flowers. 'Gloire de Lorraine', with its pink flowers, is one of the best-known varieties.

Begonia semperflorens
Low, mound-forming plant covered with small flowers all summer. Colours include shades of pink and red, as well as white, some with bronze foliage. Many varieties are offered by seed companies.

Begonia sutherlandii
Trailer with small lance-shaped leaves and a profusion of single orange flowers in loose clusters in summer.

Begonia × tuberhybrida
A group that includes large-flowered, double begonias used as both pot plants and for garden display. There are many varieties, including single and double Pendula trailers for hanging baskets, and Multifloras with masses of single, semi-double and double flowers. Colours include many shades of red, orange, pink, and yellow. All flower for many months during the summer.

HELPFUL HINTS

Temperature Aim for 13–21°C (55–70°F) for winter-flowering types. Tuberous types that die back need to be protected from frost, but only for the tubers.

Humidity High humidity is beneficial but not critical.

Position Good light, but out of direct summer sun. Provide the best possible light in winter.

Watering and feeding Water freely while the plants are in flower, cautiously at other times. Gradually withhold water from those that die

ABOVE: Begonia sutherlandii
OPPOSITE ABOVE: Begonia rex
OPPOSITE BELOW: *A group of foliage begonias. 'Cleopatra' (top left), 'Tiger' (top right), B. listada (centre), B. masoniana (bottom left), 'Red Planet' (bottom right)*

back and have a resting period once the foliage begins to yellow with age. Begonias are sensitive to over- and under-watering. Feed with a weak fertilizer while in bud and flowering.

Care Many types of begonia are prone to mildew. Spray at first sign of the disease and keep in a well-ventilated position. Pick off any affected leaves. If growing large-flowered tuberous begonias as specimen pot plants, pick off the small female flowers behind the larger and showier male blooms. Deadhead regularly except small-flowered species, which make it impractical. Tuberous varieties can be saved and overwintered in a frost-free place, but other kinds are usually discarded after flowering.

Propagation *B. semperflorens* is raised from seed. Tuberous species can be raised from cuttings in spring or by dividing old tubers (some can also be raised from seed). Winter-flowering lorraine and elatior hybrids can be propagated by leaf or tip cuttings.

Beloperone

See Justicia.

Billbergia

Terrestrial bromeliads grown for their exotic-looking flowers. The plants described are easy houseplants, and *B. nutans* is especially tolerant. Flowering time depends on the growing conditions – spring is the normal season, but if subjected to cool temperatures they may not flower until late summer.

Billbergia nutans

Arching, pendulous clusters of yellow and green, blue-edged flowers hang from conspicuous pink bracts. Foliage grows in clusters of narrow, funnel-shaped rosettes.

Billbergia × windii

A hybrid between *B. nutans* and *B. decora*. Similar to the previous species but with larger flowers and particularly conspicuous pink bracts.

ABOVE: Billbergia nutans
BELOW LEFT: Billbergia × windii

HELPFUL HINTS
Temperature Winter minimum 13°C (55°F). Lower but frost-free temperatures are unlikely to kill the plant, but it may not grow or flower so well.
Humidity Tolerates dry air if necessary.
Position Good light, but not direct sun.
Watering and feeding Water freely from spring to autumn, sparingly in winter. In summer, pour some water into the leaf rosettes, but leave these dry at other times. Feed from spring to autumn.
Care Do not discard after flowering – often the case with flowering bromeliads grown as houseplants – as new offsets flower quickly. After a few years it will make a large clump that flowers reliably every year. Repot when the clump has filled the pot.
Propagation Offsets that form around the old rosette that has flowered. Separate from the parent when the new shoots are half as tall as the parent plant.

Blechnum

Distinctive ferns with a creeping rhizome or short stem or 'trunk' (on mature plants). The leaves are arranged in a funnel-shaped rosette.

Blechnum brasiliense

Rosette of reddish-brown young fronds, maturing to green. Makes a plant up to 1m (3ft) tall.

Blechnum gibbum

Rosette of large fronds that can be up to 1m (3ft) long on a mature plant. A distinct trunk develops with age.

HELPFUL HINTS
Temperature Aim for 13–18°C (55–64°F) in winter. High winter temperatures are detrimental.
Humidity Moderate humidity.
Position Light or partial shade. Avoid exposing to direct sun.
Watering and feeding Water freely in spring and summer, moderately at other times. Never let the roots dry out. Feed with a weak fertilizer in spring and summer.
Care Remove any dead or marked fronds to keep the plant looking attractive.
Propagation Division or spores.

BELOW: Blechnum gibbum

Bougainvillea

Climbing shrubs grown for their colourful papery bracts rather than their true flowers, which are insignificant. Because of their size — 3m (10ft) or more in a border — they are better suited to a conservatory than indoors, although they can be grown successfully around hoops or supports in a small container for several years in a living-room. Besides the species and hybrids listed you will find many sold simply under varietal names, which may be varieties of the following species or be hybrids with others. They are all treated in the same way.

Bougainvillea × buttiana

A hybrid between *B. glabra* and *B. peruviana*. 'Mrs Butt' or 'Crimson Lake' are the best-known varieties, with scarlet, long-lasting, papery bracts in spring and summer. Other varieties sometimes offered include 'Miss Manila' (reddish-pink bracts), 'Mrs Helen McLean' (apricot to amber), and 'Scarlet O'Hara' (scarlet).

Bougainvillea glabra

Vigorous climber with thorny stems. Rose-red bracts in summer. There are varieties with purple to violet bracts, and 'Variegata' has variegated foliage. Varieties sometimes seen include 'Magnifica' (vivid purple), 'Rainbow' (coral red bracts becoming multicoloured as they fade), and 'Snow White' (white).

Bougainvillea spectabilis

A thorny, vigorous species, seldom grown as a houseplant. Reddish-purple bracts, but there are also varieties that are red, pink, white, and yellowish-orange.

HELPFUL HINTS

Temperature Winter minimum 13°C (55°F).

Humidity Mist regularly if in a heated room, and on hot summer days.

Position Good light. Tolerates direct sun if not too fierce, but avoid exposing to direct midday sun through glass.

Watering and feeding Water freely in summer, sparingly at other times. Avoid over-watering in spring when the new growth starts, as this may retard flowering. Feed regularly during the summer months.

Care Repot in spring if necessary. The plant rarely flowers for a second season if kept in living-room conditions, so move to a conservatory or greenhouse if possible when not in flower. Shorten the shoots in autumn to keep the plant compact, training new shoots to the support.

Propagation Cuttings.

LEFT: Bougainvillea *hybrid*
BELOW: Boungainvillea glabra *'Alexandra'*

Browallia

A small group of mainly herbaceous plants, but the one most often grown is a semi-shrubby plant usually treated like an annual and discarded when it deteriorates.

Browallia speciosa
Pale or deep blue, or white or purple flowers on bushy plants about 30cm (1ft) tall. Its varieties, rather than the species itself, are usually grown. These vary in colour and compactness, and have larger flowers than the species. Can be had in flower for most of the year by staggering the sowings.

HELPFUL HINTS
Temperature Aim for 10–15°C (50–59°F). Plants flower for longer if the temperature is not too high.

Humidity Undemanding, but mist the leaves occasionally.
Position Good light. Tolerates some direct sun, but avoid direct sun through glass during the hottest part of the day.
Watering and feeding Water freely at all times. Feed regularly.
Care Grow one plant in a 10cm (4in) pot or three in a 15cm (6in) pot. Pinch out the growing tips periodically – especially when young – to encourage bushiness. Deadhead regularly. Discard the plant when flowering has finished.
Propagation Seed in late winter or early spring for summer and autumn flowering, and in summer for winter and spring flowering.

BELOW: Browallia speciosa

Brugmansia

Likely to be found under this name or its previous name datura. The species and hybrids likely to be grown as indoor or patio plants are large shrubs. Their large size – often 1.8m (6ft) or more even if pruned back each year – makes them more appropriate for a conservatory than a living-room. All parts of these plants are potentially poisonous, so they are not a good choice if there are small children in the home.

Brugmansia × candida
Large leaves, often 30cm (1ft) or more long, and huge, bell-shaped flowers up to 20cm (8in) deep. 'Plena' has double flowers. Very fragrant. Can be in bloom throughout the year if conditions are suitable, but summer is the main flowering period. Also sold as *Datura × candida*.

Brugmansia suaveolens
Similar to the above species, with even

larger white flowers. There is a double form. Very fragrant. Also sold as *Datura suaveolens*.

HELPFUL HINTS
Temperature Winter minimum 7°C (45°F).
Humidity Undemanding, but mist the leaves occasionally.
Position Good light, preferably with some direct sun.
Watering and feeding Water freely from spring to autumn, sparingly in winter. Feed regularly from spring to autumn.
Care Prune back hard at the end of the flowering season to keep the shrub compact. If possible, grow in a tub that can be moved out to the patio for the summer and brought back indoors for the cold months.
Propagation Cuttings.

RIGHT: Brugmansia suaveolens (*syn*. Datura suaveolens)

Bryophyllum

The two viviparous species described are grown as curiosities rather than plants of beauty. They become tall and leggy with age and their appeal lies in their ability to produce plantlets along the edges or at the tips of their leaves. These can be potted up to produce new plants. If you propagate these plants frequently and discard old specimens, they make interesting plants which are easy to grow. They also make ideal houseplants for children to grow. Like other bryophyllums, they are now more correctly called *Kalanchoe*, but you will still see them sold under their old name.

Bryophyllum daigremontianum
An erect, unbranching plant to about 75cm (2½ft), with succulent leaves blotched purple beneath and plantlets around the serrated leaf edges. Also known as *Kalanchoe daigremontiana*.

Bryophyllum tubiflorum
Erect growth with cylindrical, pale reen leaves with darker markings. Plantlets are formed at the toothed ends. Also known as *Kalanchoe tubiflora*; now botanically named *K. dalagonensis*.

HELPFUL HINTS
Temperature Winter minimum 5°C (41°F).
Humidity Tolerates dry air.
Position Good light, but avoid exposing to direct summer sun.
Watering and feeding Water sparingly at all times, with enough moisture only to prevent the soil becoming completely dry in winter. Feed regularly in summer for a large plant: do no feed for a compact plant.
Care Remove plantlets that drop before they root.
Propagation Pot up the plantlets.

LEFT: Bryophyllum tubiflorum (*syn*. Kalanchoe tubiflora)

ABOVE: Bryophyllum daigremontianum (*syn*. Kalanchoe daigremontiana)

Calathea

Calatheas are exotic-looking rainforest plants, popular for their striking variegated foliage. They are demanding plants to grow in a living-room and are short-lived unless provided with sufficient warmth and humidity.

Calathea crocata
Dark green foliage with a reddish bloom, almost purple beneath the leaf. Long-lasting orange flowers.

Calathea insignis *see C. lancifolia.*

Calathea lancifolia
Lance-shaped leaves about 45 cm (1½ft) long with alternating small and large darker green blotches along each side of the main vein. The reverse side is purple. This plant is also known as *C. insignis.*

Calathea lietzei
Slightly wavy oblong leaves about 15 cm (6in) long, green with olive stripes above, reddish-purple beneath.

Calathea lubbersii
Large green leaves irregularly splashed

with flashes of yellow along each side of the main vein.

Calathea makoyana
Long stalks bearing oval papery leaves, with feathery streaks of silver and dark green blotches running from the central vein. The reverse of the leaves is purple with similar markings. This plant is also known as *Maranta makoyana.*

Calathea medio-picta
Pointed oblong leaves about 15–20 cm (6–8in) long, the upper surface dark

green with a whitish band along the central vein.

Calathea picturata
Oval, dark green leaves with white and yellowish-green streaks along the midrib and near the margins. 'Vandenheckei' has silvery streaks in the centre and on either side.

Calathea roseopicta
Large oval leaves about 20cm (8in) long, streaked pink and later fading to silvery-white. Red central vein and purplish reverse.

Calathea zebrina
Lance-shaped leaves 30–45cm (1–1½ft) long with dark green patches each side of the main vein. Grey-green or reddish-purple reverse.

HELPFUL HINTS

Temperature Winter minimum 16°C (60°F). Avoid sudden fluctuations in temperature.
Humidity Needs high humidity.
Position Partial shade or good light out of direct sun. Good light in winter, but avoid exposing to direct sun.
Watering and feeding Water freely,

FAR LEFT: Calathea crocata
OPPOSITE ABOVE: Calathea lubbersii
OPPOSITE BELOW: Calathea zebrina
ABOVE: Calathea picturata
'Vandenheckei' (left) and Calathea lancifolia *(right)*

using soft water if possible, from spring to autumn; sparingly in winter. Feed with a weak fertilizer in summer.
Care Repot annually in spring. Sponge the leaves occasionally.
Propagation Division.

Calceolaria

The only calceolarias widely grown as houseplants are hybrids, sometimes listed as *C. × herbeohybrida*. They are annuals that have to be discarded after flowering.

Calceolaria hybrids

Pouch-shaped flowers in shades of red, orange, yellow, pink, and white, usually attractively blotched or spotted. Height about 23–45cm (9–18in) according to variety. 'Grandiflora' varieties have flowers up to 6cm (2½in) across; 'Multiflora' varieties have flowers about 4cm (1½in) across. Seed companies offer many varieties.

HELPFUL HINTS
Temperature Aim for 10–15°C (50–59°F). Avoid high temperatures as much as possible.
Humidity Moderate humidity, but avoid wetting the blooms when the plant is in flower.
Position Good light, but avoid exposing to direct sun. Avoid draughts.
Watering and feeding Water freely. Never allow the plant to become dry.
Care Be alert for aphids, and spray promptly to control them if necessary. If possible, grow in a conservatory or greenhouse until just coming into flower. Discard the plant when flowering is over.
Propagation Seed in early summer. If you do not have a greenhouse or conservatory to raise plants, it is best to buy them ready-grown.

RIGHT: Calceolaria herbeo hybrida

Campanula

Most of this large group of plants are used in the herbaceous border or rock garden. *C. carpatica* is frost-hardy and best planted outdoors when flowering has finished. The other species listed here are trailing plants for the greenhouse or conservatory, but useful for short-term decoration indoors.

Campanula carpatica

Compact plant 15–23cm (6–9in) tall, covered with upward-facing, blue or white, cup-shaped flowers in summer. Often sold as a pot plant, but best planted in the garden after flowering.

Campanula fragilis

Trailing stems about 30cm (1ft) long, with blue flowers in early and mid summer.

Campanula isophylla

Trailing stems with soft blue, star-like flowers in mid and late summer. 'Mayi' has slightly larger flowers, 'Alba' is white.

HELPFUL HINTS
Temperature Winter minimum 7°C (45°F) for *C. fragilis* and *C. isophylla*. *C. carpatica* is hardy.
Humidity Undemanding, but mist the leaves occasionally.
Position Good light, but not direct summer sun.
Watering and feeding Water freely from spring to autumn, sparingly in winter.
Care Deadhead regularly. Plant *C. carpatica* in the garden when flowering is over. Cut the stems back to 5–7½cm (2–3in) at the end of the growing season to keep the plant compact and well clothed.
Propagation Seed; cuttings.

BELOW: Campanula isophylla

Capsicum

Only one species is used as a house-plant, an annual grown for its colour-ful fruits. Some varieties have round fruits, but most are cone-shaped.

Capsicum annuum

White, inconspicuous flowers in spring or summer, followed by green fruits that ripen to shades of yellow, orange, red, or purple; at their most attractive in early and mid winter.

Helpful hints
Temperature Winter minimum 13°C (55°F).
Humidity Mist the leaves regularly.
Position Good light with some direct sun.
Watering and feeding Water freely. Never allow the plant to become dry.

Care As the plant is uninteresting until the fruits ripen, keep in a green-house or conservatory if possible, and bring indoors as the fruits develop their colour. The fruits will be held for longer if kept in cool, humid conditions. Hot, dry air causes them to drop prematurely.
Propagation Seed.

Below: Capsicum annuum

Catharanthus

A small genus with a few species, only one of which is usually grown as a houseplant. Although perennial, this species is often grown as an annual.

Catharanthus roseus
Pink or white flowers about 2.5cm (1in) across with a dark eye, on compact plants that resemble the popular impatiens at a glance. Leaves have a prominent white vein. Catharanthus flower mainly between early summer and late autumn although they can be in bloom almost the year round. May also be sold as *Vinca rosea*.

HELPFUL HINTS
Temperature Minimum 10°C (50°F).
Humidity Moderate humidity.
Position Good light, but not direct sun during the hottest part of the day.
Watering and feeding Water freely at all times. Feed regularly.
Care The plant is easily raised from seed and is best discarded once it deteriorates. If you want to overwinter plants, cuttings taken in late summer will take up less space. Never let the roots become dry. Pinch out the growing tips of young plants to encourage a bushy shape.
Propagation Seed; cuttings.

BELOW: Catharanthus roseus

Caryota

ABOVE: Caryota mitis

Palms with distinctive fronds that look ragged and torn at the ends. Most caryotas make large plants given good conditions, but indoors they rarely grow to more than 1.2m (4ft).

Caryota mitis
Large fronds with individual leaflets about 15cm (6in) long and 10cm (4in) wide on a mature plant. The ends are ragged, giving a fishtail effect.

HELPFUL HINTS
Temperature Winter minimum 13°C (55°F).

Humidity Moderate humidity. Mist regularly in a centrally-heated room.
Position Good light, but avoid exposing to direct summer sun.
Watering and feeding Water freely from spring to autumn, sparingly in winter but always keep the roots slightly moist. Feed in summer.
Care Repot only when the roots have filled the pot and growth is beginning to suffer. Always ensure there is very good drainage when repotting. Sponge the leaves occasionally.
Propagation Suckers. Seed (can be difficult).

Celosia

Easy-to-grow, colourful flowering plants, often used for summer bedding outdoors but useful as a pot plant. Although strictly perennial they are almost always grown as annuals. Celosias are happier in a conservatory than in a living-room.

Celosia argentea *see C. cristata.*

Celosia cristata
Crested 'cockscomb' flowers, deeply crenated and ruffled, in shades of red, yellow, orange, and pink, in summer and early autumn. The Plumosa group has feathery flower plumes. Lance-shaped pale green leaves. The nomenclature has become confused, and you may find them listed as separate species (*C. cristata*, and *C. plumosa*) or as varieties of *C. argentea*.

Celosia plumosa *see C. cristata.*

HELPFUL HINTS
Temperature Aim for 10–15°C (50–59°F) if possible, although in summer the temperature will inevitably be

higher. Plants last better indoors than outside, and often have stronger colours if kept cool.
Humidity Moderate humidity.
Position Good light, but avoid exposing to direct summer sun through glass.
Watering and feeding Water moderately. The plant is vulnerable to both under- and over-watering. Feed regularly but cautiously: too much fertilizer with a high nitrogen content

ABOVE: Celosia cristata (*syn. C. argentea*). *These are the cockscomb type.*

may produce healthy leaves but poor flowers.
Care Discard after flowering. Best raised in a greenhouse to produce sturdy plants, but can usually be bought as young plants coming into flower.
Propagation Seed.

Cephalocereus

Ribbed, columnar cacti that rarely branch, grown mainly for the eye-catching profusion of long white hairs that they produce.

Cephalocereus chrysacanthus
Forms a large column with a green body and woolly top clothed with yellow hairs. Nine to fourteen ribs clothed with amber thorns. Red flowers are occasionally produced. Now more correctly called *Pilosocereus chrysacanthus*.

Cephalocereus senilis
Columnar growth that rarely branches, covered with long grey or white, slightly twisted hairs. Pink flowers, but these only produced on very large plants.

HELPFUL HINTS
Temperature Winter minimum 16°C (60°F).
Humidity Tolerates dry air but benefits from misting occasionally in summer.
Position Lightest possible position, benefits from direct sun.
Watering and feeding Water moderately in summer, keep almost dry in winter. Feed in spring and summer.
Care Repot only when necessary, and move into a pot only slightly larger. It may be necessary to support a tall plant with thin canes for a month or two after repotting.
Propagation Seed.

RIGHT: Cephalocereus senilis

Cereus

ABOVE: Cereus peruvianus

Columnar cacti, although in some varieties there is a disturbance of the growth point that gives them a congested and malformed appearance. In many species the flesh is covered with a whitish, green or bluish waxy layer that helps to minimize water loss through evaporation. Most are vigorous growers, and are sometimes used as rootstocks for other grafted cacti.

Cereus azureus
Upright habit with slender stems, the young ones covered with a bluish waxy bloom. The columnar stems have six or seven ribs. The large white flowers are brownish on the outside.

Cereus chalybaeus
Upright-growing columns that can be tall and 10cm (4in) across in suitable conditions, with a blue bloom. There are usually six ribs. The large flowers

are pink to red on the outside and white inside.

Cereus jamacaru
Fast-growing species with four to six ribs and stong yellowish-brown thorns. A blue waxy bloom is often noticeable. 'Monstrosus' has malformed growth that produces a mass of congested stems. Cup-shaped white flowers which open at night appear on mature plants.

Cereus peruvianus
Columnar growth with blue bloom and five to eight ribs. Clusters of sharp brown thorns, the central one up to 2cm (³⁄₄in) long. 'Monstrosus' develops a congested head of shoots that makes the plant look malformed. Old plants – often over 1m (3ft) tall – may produce flowers of 10–15cm (4–6in), red outside, white inside. The plant

sold as *C. peruvianus* is botanically considered to be *C. uruguayanus*.

HELPFUL HINTS
Temperature Winter minimum 5°C (41°F).
Humidity Tolerates dry air.
Position Lightest possible position, benefits from direct sun.
Watering and feeding Water moderately in spring and summer, very sparingly in winter.
Care Repot only when necessary. Mist occasionally to help keep the plant looking clean and fresh. The plant can be stood in the garden in summer.
Propagation Seed; cuttings (for the branching species).

Ceropegia

Over 150 species are known but only a handful are cultivated. Some species have fleshy, erect-growing stems that may be leafless, but the best-known ones are succulent trailers.

Ceropegia radicans
Creeping succulent stems that root readily, with oval to oblong succulent leaves and long, tubular flowers striped green, white, and purple-red.

Ceropegia stapeliiformis
Upright, shrubby growth with succulent stems mottled grey-brown, and only rudimentary, scale-like. Funnel-shaped greenish-white flowers blotched purple-black.

Ceropegia woodii
Wiry purplish stems, up to 1m (3ft) long, with sparse small, heart-shaped, silver-mottled leaves. Inconspicuous 1–2cm (½-¾in) pinkish tubular flowers in summer. Small tubers sometimes form on the stems. Now considered to be *C. linearis woodii*.

HELPFUL HINTS
Temperature Winter minimum 10°C (50°F).
Humidity Tolerates dry air.

ABOVE: Ceropegia woodii

Position Good light. Tolerates both full sun and partial shade.
Watering and feeding Water sparingly at all times, especially in winter. Feed regularly with a weak fertilizer in summer.
Care Shorten spindly stems that have become bare in spring.
Propagation Seed; layering; cuttings from sections of stem containing a stem tuber.

Chamaecereus

A genus of just one species, an easy-to-grow cactus that flowers readily. It is now considered by botanists to be a species of *Echinopsis* and has been called *E. chamaecereus*.

Chamaecereus silvestrii
Clump-forming, with finger-like, densely spined stems that are often decumbent and tend to trail over the edge of the pot. Funnel-shaped bright red flowers in early summer. One of the most reliable cacti for flowering.

HELPFUL HINTS
Temperature Keep cool in winter. Aim for a minimum 3°C (37°F), although it will not be killed if a couple of degrees lower.
Humidity Tolerates dry air.
Position Good light, but not direct summer sun.
Watering and feeding Water freely from spring to autumn; keep practically dry in winter. Feed regularly with a weak fertilizer from mid spring to late summer.
Care Do not over-pamper in winter. If kept cold and dry the plant may shrivel but will probably bloom all the more prolifically afterwards.
Propagation Seed; cuttings.

BELOW: Chamaecereus silvestrii

Chamaedorea

A genus of more than 100 species, but only one is widely grown as a house-plant. *C. elegans* is widely popular because of its compact size and un-demanding nature.

Chamaedorea elegans

Bright green arching leaves growing from the base. On small plants these may be only 15–30cm (6–12in) long, but on a mature plant can be 60cm (2ft) or more. Flowers, like tiny yellow balls, may appear on quite young plants. Still sometimes listed under the name *Neanthe bella*.

RIGHT: Chamaedorea elegans

HELPFUL HINTS
Temperature Aim for 12–15°C (53–59°F) in winter.
Humidity Mist the leaves occasionally, even in winter if the room is centrally-heated.
Position Good light, but avoid exposing to direct sun.
Watering and feeding Water generously from spring to autumn, but keep only just moist in winter. Feed regularly with a weak fertilizer in spring and summer.
Care Repot when its roots start to grow through the bottom of the pot. Avoid high winter temperatures as *C. elegans* benefits from a winter resting period.
Propagation Seed; division.

Chamaerops

Palms with large fan-shaped leaves. Although older specimens may be sizeable if given ideal conditions, in a large pot or tub they rarely exceed 1m (3ft). Only one species is widely grown indoors as a houseplant.

Chamaerops humilis

Fan-shaped leaves on spiny stalks on top of a short trunk on an old speci-men, but in most plants of houseplant size the trunk is missing.

HELPFUL HINTS
Temperature Aim for 3–10°C (37–50°F) in winter. Avoid high winter temperatures. Will even tolerate a few degrees of frost if the roots are dry, although this is not recommended.
Humidity Benefits from high humid-ity. Mist the leaves regularly, espe-cially in a centrally-heated room.
Position Good light, but avoid ex-posing to direct summer sun.
Watering and feeding Water gener-ously from spring to autumn. Keep fairly moist in winter if the tempera-ture is high, almost dry if cold. Feed regularly in summer.
Care Can be stood outside for the summer, after careful acclimatization. Sponge the leaves occasionally. Trim off any brown leaf tips, but do not cut into the green area. Repot young plants every two or three years.
Propagation Seed.

BELOW: Chamaerops humilis

Chlorophytum

A genus of about 200 or so species, but only a few are commonly grown as houseplants. *Chlorophytum comosum* is a native of South Africa, and it is the variegated forms that are almost exclusively used as pot plants.

Chlorophytum comosum
Linear leaves up to 2cm (¾in) wide and 30–60cm (1–2ft) long, arching to form a cascading habit. The flower stalk gradually curves as it lengthens, and as well as small star-shaped white flowers it usually bears small rosettes of leaves that form plantlets. 'Variegatum' and 'Vittatum' have white and green striped leaves.

LEFT: Chlorophytum comosum *'Vittatum'*

HELPFUL HINTS
Temperature Winter minimum 7°C (45°F). Will withstand temperatures just above freezing, but for strong, healthy plants keep them above the recommended minimum.
Humidity Undemanding, but mist the leaves occasionally.
Position Good light, but avoid exposing to direct sun.
Watering and feeding Water generously from spring to autumn, sparingly in winter. Feed regularly from spring to autumn.
Care Repot young plants annually in spring, more mature ones only when the strong, fleshy roots show signs of cracking the pot or pushing the plant from its container.
Propagation Plantlets that form on the flowering stems. Large plants can be divided.

Chrysanthemum

The florist's year-round pot chrysanthemums need no introduction. By adjusting the day length and using dwarfing chemicals, commercial growers are able to produce compact plants in flower for every season. The correct botanical name for these plants is dendranthema, but you are unlikely to find them for sale under that name. The varieties used for year-round pot chrysanthemums are derived from many species, and although named varieties are used these are seldom specified at the point of sale. There may be several plants in a single pot to produce a better display.

Year-round pot chrysanthemums
Usually less than 30cm (1ft) high when grown as a houseplant. Single and double flowers in shades of red, pink, purple, yellow, and white. Grown normally, most of these make tall plants that flower in the autumn.

HELPFUL HINTS
Temperature Aim for 10–15°C (50–59°F). Plants tolerate a warm room but the display of flowers will be much shorter-lived.
Humidity Undemanding, but mist the leaves occasionally.
Position Undemanding. As you will probably discard the plant afterwards, place in any position.
Watering and feeding Keep moist at all times. Feeding is unnecessary.
Care Deadhead to keep the plant looking tidy. Discard after flowering unless you want to try them as garden plants in which case plant out in spring or summer. Some varieties will make good tall garden plants for autumn colour, others will die – so this is a gamble.
Propagation Cuttings, although it is not practical to raise your own indoor pot chrysanthemums year-round.

BELOW: *Chrysanthemum, year-round type*

Cineraria

See Senecio cruentus.

Cissus

A large genus of tropical plants with about 350 species, some succulents, others woody. Those used most often as houseplants are vigorous climbers grown for their foliage. Any flowers that appear in summer are usually green and inconspicuous.

Cissus antarctica

Climber with woody stems and shiny oval, dark green leaves up to 10cm (4in) long. Will grow rapidly to about 3m (10ft) and needs plenty of space.

Cissus discolor

Climber with red tendrils and stems, and heart-shaped, pointed leaves that combine violet-red with silvery-grey and olive-green variegation. Flushed purplish-red beneath.

Cissus rhombifolia

Vigorous climber with dark green leaves, the undersides covered in reddish hairs. Leaves have three leaflets, the central one larger than the two behind. Still widely sold under the name *Rhoicissus rhomboidea*. 'Ellen Danica' is a widely grown variety with more deeply lobed leaflets.

HELPFUL HINTS

Temperature Aim for 7–13°C (45–55°F) in winter, with a minimum of 16°C (60°F) for *C. discolor*.

Humidity Undemanding, but mist occasionally, especially in summer.

Position Good light, but avoid exposing to direct summer sun. Provide light shade for *C. discolor*.

Watering and feeding Water generously from spring to autumn, more sparingly in winter.

Care Pinch out growing tips on young plants to stimulate new growth from low down. Keep new shoots tied to the support. Thin out overcrowded stems in spring. Spray or sponge the leaves of *C. antarctica* periodically to keep them bright and dust-free. Other species also benefit from occasional leaf-cleaning.   •

Propagation Cuttings.

TOP: Cissus rhombifolia
ABOVE: Cissus antarctica

× Citrofortunella

A hybrid genus (*Citrus* × *Fortunella*) of evergreen shrubs and trees grown mainly for their fruit. × *C. microcarpa* (syn. *Citrus mitis*) is a popular pot plant producing miniature oranges on compact plants suitable for growing indoors where larger citrus fruits would be unsuitable.

× Citrofortunella microcarpa

Glossy, dark green foliage. Small clusters of fragant white flowers, produced even on young plants, followed by miniature orange fruits about 4cm (1½in) across. These are rather bitter to taste. Summer is the usual flowering period, but both flowers and fruit may be produced almost all year round. It will reach about 1.2m (4ft) in time. May be seen under its older name of *Citrus mitis*.

× Citrofortunella mitis *see* × *C. microcarpa*.

Helpful hints

Temperature Winter minimum 10°C (50°F).
Humidity Undemanding, but mist the leaves occasionally.
Position Good light, but avoid direct summer sun through glass.
Watering and feeding Water freely in summer, sparingly in winter. Feed regularly in summer. A fertilizer containing magnesium and iron may be necessary as the plants are prone to a deficiency of these elements.
Care Stand the plants outside for the summer, afer careful acclimatization. Pollinate the flowers by dabbing with cotton wool or a small paintbrush.
Propagation Cuttings.

RIGHT: × Citrofortunella microcarpa (*syn.* Citrus mitis)

Citrus mitis

See × *Citrofortunella microcarpa*.

Clerodendrum

A large genus of about 400 mainly woody trees, shrubs and climbers, including a few that are hardy. Only *C. thomsoniae* is widely used as a houseplant, and even that is likely to prefer the conditions in a conservatory to the living-room.

Clerodendrum philippinum

Broad oval leaves up to 25cm (10in) long, and covered in hairs at the back. Fragrant white or pink flowers, at almost any time of the year.

Clerodendrum splendens

Wavy-edged, heart-shaped leaves up to 15cm (6in) long, dark green above, paler beneath. Pendulous red flower plumes between early winter and late spring.

Clerodendrum thomsoniae

Climbing stems that reach 2.4m (8ft) or more in a conservatory or greenhouse. Dark green, heart-shaped leaves. Distinctive red and white flowers in summer. The red corolla soon drops but the white calyx remains for many weeks.

Helpful hints

Temperature Aim for 13–15°C (55–59°F) in winter.
Humidity Mist the leaves regularly.
Position Good light, but not direct summer sun.
Watering and feeding Water freely spring to autumn, sparingly in winter. Feed regularly in spring and summer.
Care If required as a hanging or small bushy plant, cut back the stems by about half to two-thirds in late winter (by which time most of the foliage has probably dropped). Pinch out the growing tips of young plants if a bushy shape is required. Trail long stems around an upright support.
Propagation Cuttings; seed.

RIGHT: Clerodendrum thomsoniae

Clivia

A genus of evergreen perennials grown for their large heads of funnel-shaped flowers. Although belonging to the amaryllis family, they have fleshy, rhizomatous roots rather than a bulb. *C. miniata* is most often grown.

Clivia miniata

Large strap-shaped leaves often more than 5cm (2in) wide growing on opposite sides to create a fan-like effect. Large flower heads made of up 10–20 smaller, funnel-shaped orange or yellow flowers, in early spring.

HELPFUL HINTS

Temperature Winter minimum 10°C (50°F). Avoid warm winter temperatures.
Humidity Undemanding.
Position Good light, but avoid exposing to direct summer sun.

Watering and feeding Requires careful watering for regular blooming. Water moderately from spring to autumn, but sparingly in winter until the flower stalk is at least 15cm (6in) tall. If you water freely too soon, the leaves will grow rapidly while the flower stalk remains stunted. Be careful never to overwater as the roots are prone to rotting. Feed from flowering time to early autumn.
Care Sponge the leaves occasionally. Remove the old flower stems cutting them back as low as possible. Repot mature plants only when the roots are beginning to push the plant out from its container, and as soon as flowering is over.
Propagation Division, removing offsets with at least four leaves, after flowering.

BELOW: Clivia miniata

Cocos

A small genus, with only a couple of species that are grown as houseplants. One, the coconut palm (*C. nucifera*) is a large plant, even when young. The other (*C. weddeliana*) is a miniature palm, small enough for a table-top. Both species are difficult to keep for long periods in a living-room.

Cocos nucifera

The large seed, usually still visible when you buy the plant, indicates the large size that this palm can reach. Even indoors it will grow to 3m (10ft), but growth is slow. The fronds on a mature plant are feathery and very large, but on a young one are shaped almost like fish-tails.

Cocos weddeliana

A small palm with gracefully arching fronds of thin leaflets. It is small enough and sufficiently slow-growing to be used in a bottle garden while small. Many name changes surround this palm, and you may also find it listed or sold as *Lytocaryum weddeliana*,

ABOVE: Cocos weddeliana
LEFT: Cocos nucifera

Microcoelum weddelianum, and *Syagrus weddeliana.* Some experts now consider that it should be called *Syagrus cocoides.*

HELPFUL HINTS

Temperature Winter mimimum 18°C (64°F).

Humidity Needs high humidity.

Position Good light, ideally with some full sun, but avoid exposing to direct sun through glass during the hottest part of the day.

Watering and feeding Water freely in summer, moderately in winter. Never allow the roots to dry out. Feed with a weak fertilizer in summer.

Care Sponge the leaves occasionally, but do not use a leaf shine. Repot young plants in spring.

Propagation Seed, but this is best done by a professional grower.

Codiaeum

A small genus containing colourful evergreen trees and shrubs. Most of the plants now grown are the results of many crosses and the plants are usually classified as *C. variegatum pictum.*

There are hundreds of hybrids and varieties grouped under this name, but individual names are rarely seen on specimens sold as houseplants. Typical of the range available are 'Goldfinger' (narrow pale green leaves flushed yellow along the centre) and 'Mrs Iceton' (oval leaves, very dark and heavily marked with red and pink between the veins). 'Gold Ring' has twisted, distorted leaves.

Codiaeum variegatum pictum

Many varieties available, some with narrow, finger-like leaves, others with broad foliage; some have spiralling leaves while others are deeply lobed.

All foliage is thick, glossy, and brightly coloured or variegated; colours include green, pink, orange, red, brown, and near-black. Inconspicuous flowers, like small whitish balls, sometimes appear in summer.

HELPFUL HINTS

Temperature Winter minimum 16°C (60°F).

Humidity Needs high humidity. Mist the leaves regularly.

Position Good light, but avoid exposing to direct summer sun.

Watering and feeding Water generously from spring to autumn, sparingly in winter. Feed regularly in spring and summer.

Care Avoid cold draughts. Repot in spring, only when the plants have outgrown their existing container.

Propagation Cuttings.

BELOW: Codiaeum variegatum pictum

Colchicum

Corms with the ability to flower without soil, sometimes grown as a fun plant to flower on a windowsill in the late summer or early autumn. They are planted in the garden to grow normally once flowering indoors is over. The species described is the most common, but several other species can be treated in the same way.

Colchicum autumnale

Large crocus-shaped flowers in early autumn, usually in shades of pink. The colours are almost always paler when flowered dry indoors than when planted in the garden. The leaves do not appear until spring. Note that the corms and leaves are poisonous.

HELPFUL HINTS
Temperature Undemanding, as the plants are hardy and can be planted in the garden after flowering.
Humidity Undemanding. No special care needed.
Position A light windowsill, preferably out of strong direct sunlight.
Watering and feeding No watering or feeding necessary.
Care Place the dry corms in a saucer of sand or tray of dry pebbles to keep them upright. Set in a light position and leave the corms to flower – no water is needed. After flowering, plant in the garden in light shade, and cover with about 10cm (4in) of soil. Buy new corms each year rather than use the same ones again.
Propagation Seed; division of a large clump, but it is usually easier to buy new corms.

RIGHT: Colchicum autumnale

Coleus

A large genus of about 200 species, including perennials, annuals and evergreen sub-shrubs, many with bright and colourful foliage, but only one is widely grown. These are almost always listed as *C. blumei* hybrids, but botanists now list them as *Solenostemon* instead of coleus. However, you will almost always find them under their traditional name.

Coleus blumei hybrids

Perennial sub-shrub, but usually treated as an annual. Most have oval leaves that are gently serrated around the edge, but a few have deeply lobed foliage. Variegation varies enormously in colour and pattern, many incorporating shades of red, yellow, and green. There are named varieties, some of which have to be propagated from cuttings, but most seed mixtures produce a pleasing range of colours and patterns. Plants or cuttings are best overwintered in a greenhouse or conservatory if new stock is not to be raised from seed.

HELPFUL HINTS
Temperature Winter minimum 10°C (50°F).
Humidity Needs high humidity. Mist the leaves frequently.
Position Good light, but avoid exposing to direct summer sun during the hottest part of the day.
Watering and feeding Water freely from spring to autumn, keep the roots just moist in winter, and use soft water. Feed from spring to autumn.
Care Pinch out the growing tips of young plants to promote bushy growth. Pinch out several times more for really bushy plants. If an old plant has been overwintered, cut back hard and repot in spring to stimulate new growth from low down.

If you have raised your own plants from seed, you will probably have many, as they germinate easily. Once the plants are large enough to show their variegation clearly, retain the most appealing and discard the rest.
Propagation Seed in spring; stem cuttings in spring or summer.

RIGHT: Coleus *hybrids*

Columnea

A genus of creeping or trailing ever-green perennials or sub-shrubs, from the rain forests of Central America.

Columnea × banksii

Creeping or trailing stems with small, glossy leaves, green above and reddish beneath. Orange-red, two-lipped flowers, about 6cm (2½in) long, usually in winter and spring.

Columnea gloriosa

Long, limp, trailing stems with small leaves covered in red hairs. Scarlet flowers about 8cm (3in) long, with a yellow spot in the throat, usually in winter or spring.

Columnea hirta

Creeping or trailing stems that root readily. Red flowers about 10cm (4in) long in spring. The entire plant is covered with short, stiff hairs.

Columnea microphylla

Long, thin, trailing stems up to 1m (3ft) in length, with small almost circular leaves. Orange-red flowers in spring or summer.

HELPFUL HINTS

Temperature Winter minimum 13°C (55°F).

Humidity Needs high humidity. Mist the leaves regularly.

Position Good light, but avoid exposing to direct summer sun.

Watering and feeding Water freely from spring to autumn, sparingly in winter. Feed regularly in spring and summer months.

Care Shorten the stems once flowering is over to keep the plant compact. Repot every second or third year.

Columneas do best planted in the humus-rich fibrous compost (potting soil) sold for bromeliads and orchids.
Propagation Cuttings.

TOP: Columnea microphylla
BOTTOM: Columnea gloriosa
MIDDLE: Columnea hirta

Cordyline

Evergreen shrubs and trees grown mainly for their foliage. Some of the species are sometimes sold as dracaenas, and there is often confusion between these two genera. If in doubt about whether a particular plant is a cordyline or a dracaena, check the roots. Cordylines have creeping roots that are knobbly and white when cut, while dracaenas have non-creeping roots that are smooth and yellow or orange if cut.

Cordyline australis
Sword-shaped green leaves that can be 1m (3ft) long. Some varieties are variegated, with red or yellow stripes along the green leaves. *C. a.* 'Purpurea' has reddish-purple leaves. Young plants grown indoors usually lack a distinctive trunk, which only develops on older plants. Young plants in the home are unlikely to flower.

Cordyline fruticosa
Old plants develop a clear stem or trunk, and grow large, but the young specimens usually sold as houseplants are leafy down to the base and remain compact for a long time. The species itself has plain green leaves, but there

ABOVE LEFT: Cordyline australis
ABOVE: Cordyline terminalis (*syn.* C. fruticosa) '*Kiwi*'

are many variegated varieties, heavily marked with red, pink, or cream, and sometimes a combination of these colours. Some have broad leaves, others narrower ones. Treat them all in the same way. This plant can be sold as *C. terminalis* or *Dracaena terminalis*.

Cordyline terminalis *see C. fruticosa.*

HELPFUL HINTS
Temperature Winter minimum 13°C (55°F) for tender species such as *C. fruticosa*, 3°C (37°F) for tough species such as *C. australis*.
Humidity *C. australis* is undemanding. Tropical species such as *C. fruticosa* require high humidity and should be misted regularly.
Position Good light, but avoid exposing to direct sun. *C. australis* will tolerate direct sun, but avoid summer sun through glass during the hottest part of the day.
Watering and feeding Water freely from spring to autumn, sparingly in winter. Feed tropical species regularly in spring and summer, *C. australis* less frequently.

Care Sponge leaves occasionally to remove dust and make them look brighter. Repot every second spring. *C. australis* and its varieties make attractive patio plants for the summer, but acclimatize them to outdoor conditions first. In mild areas where frosts are never severe they are sometimes successful when planted permanently in the garden, but they are best regarded as frost-tender, especially young plants.
Propagation Cuttings and stem sections with an eye, rooted in a propagator, are the best ways to increase the number of plants. An old specimen that has become leggy where leaves have fallen can be air layered.

Crassula

A large genus of about 300 succulents, ranging from dwarfs of less than 2.5cm (1in) to tall species over 5m (16ft). The species listed are just a selection of those sometimes grown as house and conservatory plants.

Crassula arborescens
Tree-shaped and will grow to about

BELOW: Crassula argentea

ABOVE: Crassula lycopodiodes
RIGHT: Crassula arborescens

1.8m (6ft) if conditions are suitable. Thick, greyish leaves edged with a red margin. White flowers, fading to pink, may appear in early and mid summer on a mature plant.

Crassula argentea *see C. portulacea.*

Crassula ovata *see C. portulacea.*

Crassula portulacea
Tree-shaped with a short 'trunk'. May grow to 1m (3ft) or more. Thick dark green succulent leaves about 2.5–5cm (1–2in) across, edged red. You may also find the plant under two other names: *C. argentea* and *C. ovata.*

Crassula lycopodioides
Distinctive fleshy stems forming an upright cluster, completely covered with minute fleshy, scale-like leaves arranged in four rows. Tiny greenish-yellow flowers in spring. The correct botanical name for this plant is now *C. mucosa.*

HELPFUL HINTS
Temperature Aim for 7–10°C (45–50°F) in winter. Avoid high temperatures in winter, otherwise the plants become lanky and leaves may fall.
Humidity Tolerates dry air.
Position Good light, in sun if possible. Species with very pale green leaves or a white bloom are best protected from strong direct sunlight through glass.

Watering and feeding Water sparingly at all times, and keep almost dry in winter. Feed with a weak fertilizer occasionally in summer.
Care Repot annually in spring while the plants are still young. Restrict watering for a while after repotting, otherwise the roots may rot.
Propagation Leaf and tip cuttings. Seed is an option but seldom used.

Crocus

Mainly spring-flowering corms, but some bloom in the autumn. It is the popular spring-flowering kinds that are almost exclusively used indoors.

Crocus chrysanthus
Typical crocus-shaped flowers, but smaller and earlier than the large-flowered varieties. The true species is seldom grown, but there are many varieties in a range of colours available for autumn planting. They bloom indoors in late winter. The grass-like leaves have a white central stripe.

Crocus, large-flowered
The typical large-flowered crocuses of spring, botanically derived from *C. vernus.* Grass-like leaves with a white

central stripe. There are many varieties to plant in autumn for late winter and early spring blooming.

HELPFUL HINTS
Temperature Keep cool. Leave in the garden until mid winter but protect from excessive freezing in cold climates, also rain that might waterlog the pots or containers. Maintain in cool conditions indoors until at least a third of the developing flower bud is visible.
Humidity Undemanding.
Position Good light once brought indoors. A sunny position will encourage the flowers to open fully.
Watering and feeding Water cautiously so that the corms do not start to rot.
Care After flowering, plant in the garden. Do not attempt to force the same corms for a second time – buy new ones each year.
Propagation Small offset corms; seed. Crocuses are seldom propagated by amateurs because it takes several years to produce plants of flowering size. It is more convenient to buy flowering-sized corms.

BELOW: Crocus, *large-flowered hybrid*

ABOVE: Crossandra infundibuliformis

Crossandra

A genus of tropical evergreen sub-shrubs with long-lasting, attractive flowers. Several species are grown as houseplants, but the one described here is the most commonly found.

Crossandra infundibuliformis
Bright heads of tubular soft orange flowers about 2.5cm (1in) across above glossy, dark green, oval to lance-shaped leaves. The plants flower while still young and may be in bloom from mid spring to autumn if conditions suit. Most plants reach about 30–60cm (1–2ft) indoors. Sometimes sold under its old name of *C. undulifolia*.

Crossandra undulifolia *see C. infundibuliformis*.

HELPFUL HINTS
Temperature Winter minimum 13°C (55°F).
Humidity High humidity is essential. Mist the leaves regularly.
Position Good light, but avoid exposing to direct summer sun.
Watering and feeding Water gener-

ously in summer, less often in winter.
Care Deadhead regularly to prolong season of flowering. Repot in spring if necessary.
Propagation Stem cuttings; seed (used commercially but difficult in the home).

Cryptanthus

Genus of rosette-forming bromeliads, grown for their attractive foliage. The colouring often varies according to the light intensity.

Cryptanthus acaulis
Low-growing rosette of green, narrow, pointed leaves about 10–15cm (4–6in) long, the edges wavy and slightly serrated. Fragrant tubular white flowers sometimes appear from the centre of each rosette in summer.

Cryptanthus bromelioides
Large rosettes about 20cm (8in) or more tall, with strap-shaped and finely toothed green leaves. White flowers are occasionally produced, usually in summer. More decorative is *C. b. tricolor*, which is suffused with carmine and striped white.

Cryptanthus zonatus
Flattish rosettes of wavy leaves about 20cm (8in) long, cross-banded dark sepia-green and silvery-white. A clus-

BELOW: Cryptanthus bromeliodes tricolor

ter of white flowers may be produced from the centre of rosettes in summer.

HELPFUL HINTS

Temperature Winter minimum 18°C (64°F).

Humidity Needs high humidity.

Position Good light, but not direct summer sun.

Watering and feeding Water freely in spring and summer, cautiously in autumn and sparingly in winter. Never allow the roots to dry out. Pour water into the rosettes in summer, but not in winter. Try to use tepid water. Feed regularly with a weak fertilizer in summer.

Care If the plant has to be repotted, choose a shallow container as cryptanthus have a shallow root system. Can also be grown as epiphytes in a basket or on a piece of bark. Old rosettes die once they have flowered, but young ones (offsets) will have formed around the centre of the old plants.

Propagation Offsets or plantlets which grow from the centre of the old plant in these species.

Ctenanthe

ABOVE: Ctenanthe lubbersiana
RIGHT: Ctenanthe oppenheimiana

Evergreen perennials, mainly from Brazil, grown for their attractive foliage. The two species listed here are the ones most likely to be sold as houseplants.

Ctenanthe lubbersiana

Clump-forming with almost oblong leaves, about 20–25cm (8–10in) long, and on long stalks that end in an abrupt point. The leaves are irregularly splashed with pale yellow above, pale green below. Grows to about 60–75cm (2–2½ft) as a houseplant.

Ctenanthe oppenheimiana

Densely leaved, clump-forming plant with leaves usually more than 30cm (1ft) long, on tall stems that produce a plant about 1m (3ft) tall. The foliage is dark green above with irregular silvery-white bands each side of the midribs, and reddish-purple beneath. 'Tricolor' has large cream blotches over the green leaves.

HELPFUL HINTS

Temperature Winter minimum 16°C (60°F).

Humidity Needs high humidity.

Position Good light, but avoid exposing to direct sun.

Watering and feeding Water moderately at all times. Do not water if the surface is still damp, but never let the roots dry out. Use soft water if possible – for watering and misting. Feed in summer.

Care Sponge leaves occasionally to remove dust and to keep them looking bright. Cut out any leaves that have deteriorated.

Propagation Division.

ABOVE: Cyclamen, *large-flowered hybrid*

Watering and feeding Water freely while the plants are growing actively. Gradually reduce the amount of water given once flowering has finished. During the resting period give just a little water occasionally to prevent the corm shrivelling. Feed regularly during the active growing and flowering periods.

Care Deadhead regularly, trying not to leave any stumps of flower stalk as these will be prone to rotting. Once the leaves have died, the corm goes into a dormant period, so keep the pot in a cool place (perhaps outside) and almost dry until mid summer. Then start watering again (repot if necessary, burying the tuber to half its depth), and bring indoors if the plant has been in the garden during the summer months.

Propagation Seed. Most varieties take 15–18 months to flower, but miniature cyclamen can be in flower in about 8 months.

Cyclamen

A small genus that includes hardy species with tiny flowers as well as the more popular florist's cyclamen. Those grown as pot plants are derived from *C. persicum*, which is native to the Middle East.

Cyclamen persicum
The species itself is not grown, but its hybrids and varieties are available in a range of pinks, reds, purples, salmon and white. The wide, reflexed petals are sometimes frilled or ruffled, and some of the varieties are fragrant. Leaf patterning is also variable, and often marbled or zoned white or silver. The main flowering time is autumn to early spring. Standard varieties grow to about 30cm (1ft), intermediate ones to about 23cm (9in), and miniatures to 15cm (6in) or less.

HELPFUL HINTS
Temperature Aim for 10–15°C (50–59°F) in winter. High temperatures will shorten the flowering period.
Humidity Moderate humidity. Plants benefit from misting when only foliage is present, but be careful not to spray the flowers. Humidity is best provided by standing the pot on pebbles over water.
Position Good light, but avoid exposing to direct sun.

Cymbidium

A genus of 45 or so species, including both epiphytes and semi-terrestrial orchids. There are a great many hybrids, and it is these that are normally grown in the home, where they are among the most reliable orchids to grow as houseplants.

Cymbidium hybrids
Upright spikes of large waxy-looking flowers, in colours such as green, yellow, pink, and white, usually attractively speckled or marked. Flowering time is usually between autumn and spring. Many named hybrids are grown by specialist orchid nurseries, but variety names may not be identified if you buy from a garden centre or superstore. However, all those widely sold as pot plants can be treated in the same way.

HELPFUL HINTS
Temperature Aim for 7–13°C (45–55°F) in winter.

Humidity Mist the leaves regularly. Humidity is best provided by standing the pot on pebbles over water.
Position Good light, but avoid exposing to direct sun.
Watering and feeding Water freely in spring and summer, sparingly in autumn and winter. Never let the roots dry out. Use soft, tepid water if possible. Feed during the flowering period.
Care Avoid a stuffy position and provide ventilation whenever it is warm enough. The plants – which are uninteresting out of flower – can be stood in a sheltered position outdoors for the summer. Repot only when the existing pot is full of roots, and use a special orchid mixture if possible.
Propagation Commercial growers use micropropagation but the easiest method for an amateur is division of an established clump, ideally after flowering.

BELOW: Cymbidium *hybrid*

Cyperus

A large genus with more than 600 species of rush-like plants, a few of which are grown as houseplants. They are a good choice for anyone who tends to overwater their plants, as they will actually thrive if the pot stands in a little water.

Cyperus albostriatus
Sedge with grass-like leaves, radiating out like the ribs of an opened umbrella, at the top of stems about 60cm (2ft) tall. This is the plant often grown as *C. diffusus*. 'Variegatus' has white-striped leaves.

Cyperus alternifolius
Grass-like leaves radiate from stiff stalks, resembling the ribs of an open umbrella. 'Variegatus' has white stripes along the length of its leaves. Height about 1m (3ft). Now more correctly called *C. involucratus*, but the name under which it is listed here is

ABOVE: Cyperus alternifolius

the one by which you are likely to purchase it.

Cyperus diffusus *see C. albostriatus*.

Cyperus involucratus *see C. alternifolius*.

HELPFUL HINTS
Temperature Winter minimum 7°C (45°F).
Humidity Mist the leaves regularly.
Position Good light, but not direct summer sun.
Watering and feeding Water freely at all times. Keep the roots moist. It will not matter if the pot stands in a little water. Feed from mid spring to early autumn.
Care Cut out any yellowing stems. Repot every spring.
Propagation Division.

Cypripedium

See Paphiopedilum.

Datura

See Brugmansia.

Davallia

A genus of evergreen or semi-evergreen, often epiphytic, ferns from tropical areas of Asia and Australia.

Davillia bullata

Divided fronds about 30cm (12in) long, sometimes with a puckered appearance.

Davallia fejeensis

A small to medium-sized fern with layers of delicate lacy fronds. Creeping rhizomes on the surface often grow over the edge of the pot.

HELPFUL HINTS

Temperature Winter minimum 7°C (45°F).
Humidity Mist the leaves regularly.
Position Partial shade or good light without direct sun.
Watering and feeding Water freely from spring to autumn, more sparingly in winter.
Care Remove dying or fading fronds.
Propagation Division; spores.

BELOW: Davallia bullata

Dendranthema

See Chrysanthemum.

Dieffenbachia

Bold foliage plants with poisonous or irritant sap that should be kept away from mouth, eyes and skin. The nomenclature of some dieffenbachias has become very confused, and you may find them sold under several synonyms. Many of the hybrids are listed simply under varietal name. As they can all be treated in the same way, this is not especially important horticulturally.

Dieffenbachia amoena

Large oblong leaves, often 60cm (2ft) long, on a thick stem. Dark green foliage with cream or white marbling along the side veins. 'Tropic Snow' is an example of a variety with heavier white variegation. You might find *D. amoena* listed as a variety of *D. seguine*, which is where some botanists now prefer to place it.

Dieffenbachia × bausei

Yellowish-green leaves about 30cm (1ft) long, marbled dark green with white patches.

Dieffenbachia bowmannii

Varieties of this species have dark and light flecks on the body of the leaves, overlaid with white or cream. The leaves can be up to 75cm (2½ft) long. There are varieties with bolder white variegation.

Dieffenbachia maculata

Large oval leaves up to 60cm (2ft) long and 20cm (8in) wide with ivory or cream blotches and markings – the variegation depending on the variety. 'Camilla' and 'Exotica' are popular varieties. For many years this species has been considered synonymous with *D. picta*.

Dieffenbachia picta *see D. maculata.*

TOP: Dieffenbachia maculata *'Camilla'*
ABOVE: Dieffenbachia maculata *'Exotica'*

Dieffenbachia seguine *see D. amoena.*

HELPFUL HINTS

Temperature Winter minimum 16°C (60°F).
Humidity Mist the leaves regularly.
Position Partial shade or good light without direct summer sun. Good light without direct sun in winter.
Watering and feeding Water freely from spring to autumn, sparingly in winter.
Care Wash leaves occasionally. Repot each spring. If the plant has become

bare at the base, try pruning back to leave a stump of about 15cm (6in) – it will often respond by producing new shoots.

Propagation Cane cuttings or stem cuttings. Air layering is a useful method for plants that have become bare at the base.

Dionaea

Insectivorous, rosette-forming perennials. The species described here is most widely sold as a fun plant. It does not make a good houseplant, however, and will probably die in a short time in a living-room.

Dionaea muscipula

Rosettes of modified hinged leaves fringed with large hairs along the edges. Insects landing on the plant can trigger the trap, which snaps closed. The two halves open again when the insect has been digested.

HELPFUL HINTS

Temperature Aim for 3–10°C (37–50°F) in winter. Keep plants frost-free, but avoid exposing to high temperatures.

Humidity High humidity is essen-

BELOW: Dionaea muscipula

tial. Mist regularly, and if possible provide additional humidity by other methods.

Position Good light, even direct sunlight, provided plants are screened from sun through glass during the hottest part of the day in summer. Best possible light in winter – supplementary artificial lighting can be beneficial, but should be of the type specially designed for use with plants.

Watering and feeding Keep constantly moist. Do not feed.

Care Repot, if necessary, in spring but use an ericaceous compost (potting soil) (one for acid-loving plants) and mix with an equal volume of chopped sphagnum moss (the type used to line hanging baskets). Cover the surface with more moss.

Propagation Seed; division.

Dizygotheca

A genus of small evergreen trees and shrubs, the species below being the only one widely used as a houseplant.

Dizygotheca elegantissima

Graceful plant with dark green,

ABOVE: Dizygotheca elegantissima

almost black, leaves divided into seven to eleven finger-like serrated leaflets. On mature plants the leaflets tend to be broader, which alters their appearance slightly. In the home it will often make a plant 1–1.2m (3–4ft) tall. The plant used to be known as *Aralia elegantissima*, and some experts consider there is confusion among the plants in cultivation between this species and *Schefflera elegantissima*. However, you are most likely to find it sold as a dizygotheca.

HELPFUL HINTS

Temperature Winter minimum 13°C (55°F).

Humidity Mist the leaves regularly.

Position Good light; not direct summer sun at the hottest part of the day.

Watering and feeding Water moderately from spring to autumn, sparingly in winter.

Care Repot every second spring. If the plant becomes leggy, try cutting it down to about 10cm (4in) – it may be stimulated into producing new shoots from the base.

Propagation Seed or air layering in spring. Tip cuttings in summer.

Dracaena

The genus dracaena contains many species of palm-like plants from Africa and Asia, most of them creating the impression of an exotic plant while actually being quite tough. This has made them very popular indoor plants. The genus is sometimes confused with cordylines, but the dracaenas on the whole have less spectacularly coloured leaves and they rely on simple but very striking variegation and bold outline for their attraction. *D. godseffiana* is the odd one out, being distinctly shrubby and bearing oval rather than strap-shaped leaves.

Dracaena deremensis

Stalkless sword-shaped leaves growing directly from an upright stem. 'Janet Craig' is an all-green variety, but mostly the variegated varieties are grown. These include varieties with light or dark green leaves, and white, silver, yellow, or green stripes. Two well-known examples are 'Bausei' (white stripes on a dark green background), and 'Warneckii' (green and white central band and narrow white lines along the margins).

Dracaena fragrans

Similar to the previous species but the leaves are longer and broader and a distinct trunk forms even on young plants. The attractively variegated varieties are usually grown, such as 'Massangeana' (yellowish-green stripes along the centre of the leaf). The heavily scented flowers are unlikely to form on small plants in the home.

Dracaena godseffiana

Shrubby growth with pointed oval leaves on thin stems. The glossy green foliage is splashed and mottled with cream, but the colouring and extent of the variegation depends on the variety. Makes a bushy plant about 60cm (2ft) high, and flowers at an early age. These flowers are yellowish-green and fragrant, and may be followed by attractive red berries.

Dracaena marginata

Narrow trunk, often twisted; unbranched on young plants but in time may become branched and tall (perhaps to ceiling height). Narrow green leaves, edged purplish-red, 30–45cm (1–1½ft) or more long. More brightly coloured varieties include 'Colorama' (broad red band along each edge) and 'Tricolor' (green, cream, and red).

Dracaena sanderiana

Oval to lance-shaped leaves about 23cm (9in) long, edged with a broad creamy-white band.

Dracaena surculosa *see D. godseffiana.*

Dracaena terminalis *see Cordyline fruticosa.*

HELPFUL HINTS

Temperature Winter minimum 13°C (55°F); 10°C (50°F) for *D. godseffiana* and *D. sanderiana.*

Humidity Mist the leaves regularly. *D. godseffiana* tolerates dry air.
Position Good light, but avoid exposing to direct sun.
Watering and feeding Water freely from spring to autumn, sparingly in winter. Never let the roots dry out. Feed regularly in spring and summer.
Care Sponge the leaves occasionally to keep them clean and bright. Cease feeding by autumn to help give the plant a resting period of less active growth. Repot in spring if necessary.
Propagation Tip cuttings; air layering (for a leggy plant); cane cuttings.

BELOW: Dracaena deremensis (right), and two of its varieties: 'Yellow Stripe' (centre) and 'White Stripe' (left)
OPPOSITE ABOVE: Dracaena sanderiana
OPPOSITE MIDDLE: Dracaena fragrans (right) and D.f. 'Massageana' (left)
OPPOSITE BELOW: Dracaena godseffiana
FAR RIGHT: Dracaena marginata (right) and D.m. 'Tricolor' (left)

Echeveria

Rosette-forming succulents, grown mainly for their often attractive shape and colouring. Most species will flower, and although the flowers are not especially beautiful they are sufficiently appealing in most species to be a bonus. Of the more than 150 species and many hybrids, the ones listed below are just examples.

Echeveria elegans
Rosettes of fleshy bluish-white leaves up to 15cm (6in) across. Pink or red flowers, tipped yellow, from early spring to mid summer. Its correct botanical name is *E. secunda glanca*.

Echeveria glauca
Rosettes of waxy, spoon-shaped, blue-grey leaves. Yellow flowers tinged red in spring and early summer.

Temperature Aim for 5–10°C (41–50°F) in winter.
Humidity Tolerates dry air.
Position Best possible light throughout the year. Will tolerate full sun.
Watering and feeding Water moderately from spring to autumn. Give enough water in winter to prevent the leaves shrivelling. Feed in spring and summer using a weak fertilizer.
Care Avoid getting water on the leaves if possible (it may damage the waxy layer and lead to rotting). Avoid high winter temperatures. If most of the lower leaves drop in winter, use the tips as cuttings and start again.
Propagation Tip cuttings; leaf cuttings; offsets (if the rosette produces them); seed.

LEFT: Echeveria elegans
BELOW LEFT: Echeveria glauca

Echinocactus

Slow-growing spherical to cylindrical cacti, usually with fierce but attractive spines. The plants rarely flower in cultivation.

Echinocactus grusonii
The best-known species, spherical when young, slightly more cylindrical

BELOW: Echinocactus grusonii

with age. Very old specimens in bota-
nic gardens can be 1m (3ft) across, but
in the home they usually remain small.

HELPFUL HINTS
Temperature Aim for 5–10°C (41–
50°F) in winter.
Humidity Tolerates dry air.
Position Best possible light throughout the year. Tolerates full sun.
Watering and feeding Water moderately from spring to autumn, keep
practically dry in winter. Feed with a
weak fertilizer in spring and summer.
Care Repot only as necessary, and
always use a special cactus mixture.
Be careful because the roots are easily
damaged.
Propagation Seed.

Echinocereus

Spherical to columnar cacti, freely
branched with age. Different species
vary considerably in appearance –
some are practically bare, others are
densely thorned or hairy.

Echinocereus pectinatus
Columnar growth with numerous ribs
and small spines that are yellow at first
but later become grey. Sometimes
sparsely branched. Flowers freely in
spring, with trumpet-shaped purple,

BELOW: Echinocereus salm-dyckianus

ABOVE: Echinocereus pectinatus

pink, or yellow blooms about 12cm
(5in) across.

Echinocereus salm-dyckianus
Dark green stems, branching at the
base, covered with yellowish thorns
tipped red. Produces its orange flowers
freely in spring. This is now considered by botanists to be more correctly
named *E. scheeri*.

HELPFUL HINTS
Temperature Aim for 10–13°C (50–
55°F) in winter.
Humidity Tolerates dry air, but
appreciates higher humidity than
most cacti.
Position Best possible light throughout the year. Tolerates full sun.
Watering and feeding Water moderately from spring to autumn. Keep
practically dry in winter. Feed regularly in spring and summer with a
weak fertilizer.
Care Repot only when necessary, using a cactus mixture.
Propagation Cuttings if the species
produces a sideshoot; seed.

Echinopsis

Spherical cacti, sometimes slightly
columnar; generally freely branching.

Echinopsis eyriesii
Spherical at first, becoming more columnar with age. Numerous ribs with
dark brown spines. Large, tubular,
greenish-white scented flowers in
spring or summer.

Echinopsis rhodotricha
Globular or columnar stems with
2.5cm (1in) long pale yellow spines
tipped brown. Large white flowers in
summer.

HELPFUL HINTS
Temperature Aim for 5–10°C (41–
50°F) in winter.
Humidity Tolerates dry air.
Position Good light, but screen from
very intense direct sunlight.
Watering and feeding Water moderately from spring to autumn. Keep
practically dry in winter. Feed with a
weak fertilizer in spring and summer.
Care Repot as necessary, using a cactus mixture. Avoid turning the plant
when coming into flower (after
flowering it does not matter). It is
common for the flowers to develop on
the shady side.
Propagation Seed; cuttings.

BELOW: Echinopsis eyriesii

Epiphyllum

Genus of cacti with strap-shaped leaves, mainly from Central and South America and especially Mexico. The plants that are grown in the home, however, are almost always hybrids.

Epiphyllum hybrids

Erect, flattened, or triangular stems, sometimes winged or with a wavy edge, spreading outwards with age and often requiring support. Very large funnel-shaped flowers with a wide-flared mouth, in spring and early summer. Mainly in shades of red and pink, as well as white.

HELPFUL HINTS

Temperature Aim for 7–10°C (45–50°F) in winter. Avoid high winter temperatures.

Humidity Undemanding, but benefits from misting in spring and summer.

Position Good light, but avoid exposing to direct sun.

Watering and feeding Water freely from spring to autumn, sparingly in winter. Use soft water if possible. Feed regularly in spring and summer.

Care The plants are uninteresting out of flower so you may prefer to stand them in the garden for the summer. Avoid moving the plants once buds form, otherwise they may drop.

Propagation Cuttings.

BELOW: Epiphyllum *hybrids*

ABOVE: Epipremnum aureum (*syn.* Scindapsus aureus)

Epipremnum

Woody climbers. The most popular species, described below, is often used in the home as a trailing plant.

Epipremnum aureum

Climber with aerial roots and heart-shaped glossy leaves, blotched or streaked with yellow. There are attractive variegated varieties such as 'Marble Queen' (white and green), and golden forms such as 'Neon'. This plant has been subject to several name-changes, and although you will find it in some shops and garden centres under the name given here, you will also find it sold as *Scindapsus aureus,* and it is sometimes listed as *Rhaphidophora aurea.*

HELPFUL HINTS

Temperature Winter minimum 13°C (55°F).

Humidity Undemanding, but benefits from occasional misting.

Position Good light, but avoid exposing to direct sun. Usually does well in poor light, but variegation is much improved in good light.

Watering and feeding Water freely from spring to autumn, sparingly in

winter. Feed in spring and summer.
Care Repot in spring if necessary.
Long shoots can be shortened to keep
the plant compact.
Propagation Leaf bud or stem tip
cuttings; layering.

Erica

A very large genus of over 500 species,
many of them hardy plants used in the
garden, but only the two described
here are the ones most commonly used
as houseplants.

BELOW: Erica gracilis
BOTTOM: Erica hiemalis

Erica gracilis
Leafy spike of urn-shaped pink flowers
with white tips, in winter. The plant
grows to about 30cm (1ft). Needle-
like foliage.

Erica hyemalis
Small white, pink, or reddish bell-
shaped flowers on spikes with needle-
like leaves, in winter. Grows to about
30cm (1ft).

HELPFUL HINTS
Temperature Aim for 5–13°C (41–
55°F) during flowering period.
Humidity Mist the leaves regularly.
Position Good light. Will benefit
from winter sun.
Watering and feeding Water freely
at all times. Never allow the roots to
dry out. Use soft water if possible.
Care These are not practical plants to
keep in the home long-term, and are
usually bought in flower. Cool
temperatures will prolong flowering,
after which the plants are usually
discarded. They can sometimes be
kept successfully for another year by
trimming back the shoots after
flowering and keeping in a cool, light
position until early summer. Stand
the pot outdoors for the summer and
bring in again before the first frost.
Propagation Cuttings.

Euonymus

A genus that includes many hardy
trees and shrubs, and the species sometimes grown as a houseplant is a common hardy garden shrub. The variegated varieties make acceptable pot
plants for an unheated room or for a
cold porch, and these varieties can be
planted in the garden once they
become too large.

Euonymus japonicus
Oval leaves on upright stems, the
upper surface dark green and glossy,
the underside paler. The more attractive and less vigorous variegated
varieties are the ones usually grown

indoors, such as the small-leaved
'Microphyllus Albovariegatus' (white
variegation), and 'Microphyllus Aureo-
variegatus' (gold and green).

HELPFUL HINTS
Temperature Aim for 3–7°C (37–
45°F) in winter, although plants
should survive even if it drops below
freezing.
Humidity Undemanding, but mist
the leaves occasionally.
Position Good light, with or without
direct sun.
Watering and feeding Water freely
from spring to autumn, sparingly in
winter. Feed regularly in spring and
summer.
Care It is a good idea to stand the
plants in the garden for the summer
months, to keep the growth sturdy
and the variegation strong.
Propagation Cuttings.

BELOW: Euonymus japonicus
'Mediopictus'

Euphorbia

There are about 2,000 species of euphorbia ranging from annuals to shrubs, hardy border plants to tender houseplants including the poinsettia (*E. pulcherrima*). Others, such as *E. milii,* are succulents.

Euphorbia milii
Succulent shrub with woody and very thorny stems, bearing inconspicuous true flowers surrounded by bold, bright red bracts. Flowering time is spring to mid summer. The plant can grow to about 1m (3ft), but it will remain compact for many years. The sap is poisonous. May also be found under its old name of *E. splendens*.

Euphorbia obesa
Unusual-looking spherical succulent, dark green often chequered with light green, with eight flat ribs dividing the body in sections from top to bottom. A crown of cup-shaped, greenish-yellow flowers in summer.

Euphorbia pulcherrima
Erect shrubby plant grown for its colourful red, pink, or white bracts in winter (the true flowers are insignificant). Most plants bought in flower are a compact 30–60cm (1–2ft) but dwarfing chemicals will have been used. If you keep the plant for another season it will be taller.

Euphorbia splendens *see E. milii.*

Euphorbia trigona
Candelabrum-shaped succulent with triangular or winged stems. Pale green stem markings. Small oval leaves that are deciduous.

HELPFUL HINTS
Temperature Winter minimum 13°C (55°F) for most species, although the succulent kinds will usually tolerate temperatures of 10°C (50°F) quite happily.
Humidity High humidity for *E. pulcherrima* – mist the leaves regularly.

ABOVE: Euphorbia milii
ABOVE LEFT: Euphorbia trigona
LEFT: Euphorbia obesa

Succulent species tolerate dry air, but mist *E. milii* occasionally in spring and summer.
Position Best possible light for all species in winter, but avoid direct summer sun for *E. pulcherrima*. Succulent species tolerate direct sun.
Watering and feeding Water succulent species freely from spring to autumn, sparingly in winter. Water *E. pulcherrima* freely when in flower and in summer, moderately at other times but never let the roots dry out. Feed succulent species with a weak fertilizer in summer; feed *E. pulcherrima* in sum-mer and until it is in full flower.
Care Succulent varieties need little extra care apart from repotting when it becomes necessary. *E. pulcherrima* needs careful cultivation if it is to flower another year. Cut back the stems to leave 10cm (4in) stumps when flowering is over, and keep the roots only just moist, to induce a resting period. Repot in late spring and start watering more freely, feeding regularly as new growth is stimulated. Thin excess stems to leave about four or five on each plant. To induce flowering in early winter again, control the amount of light received from early or mid autumn. Eliminate light (using a black plastic sack, for instance) for 14 hours each day. Put the cover on in the evening and remove the next morning. Continue this treatment for eight weeks, then grow the plant on normally.
Propagation Cuttings of *E. pulcherrima* and *E. milii*. Seed is the best method for the other succulent species mentioned.

Eustoma

A genus of annuals and perennials with poppy-like flowers. The species listed is often grown as a cut flower but can also be found as a pot plant.

Eustoma grandiflorum

Open, poppy-like flowers in shades of blue, pink, and white, in summer. There are also double varieties. Small lance-shaped green leaves, about 5cm (2in) long. Compact varieties that grow to about 30–45cm (1–1½ft) are best for pots. Other names are *Lisianthus russellianus* and *E. russellianum*.

BELOW: Eustoma grandiflorum (*syn.* Lisianthus russellianus)

HELPFUL HINTS
Temperature Winter minimum 7°C (45°C).
Humidity Mist occasionally.
Position Good light, but avoid direct summer sun.
Watering and feeding Water with care at all times, making sure the compost (potting soil) never becomes dry or waterlogged. Feed regularly once the nutrients in the initial potting soil become depleted.
Care Although technically perennials, these plants are treated as annuals and discarded when flowering has finished.
Propagation Seed. Plants can be divided in autumn, but it is more satisfactory to raise fresh ones from seed.

ABOVE: Exacum affine

Exacum

A genus of about 40 species, including annuals, biennials and perennials. Only one species, however, is now widely grown, mainly because it is so easy to raise from seed and because it flowers well in a pot.

Exacum affine

Masses of small, pale purple (sometimes white), slightly fragrant flowers with yellow centres. The main flowering period is from mid summer to late autumn. Small, fresh green leaves 2–4cm (¾–1½in) long.

HELPFUL HINTS
Temperature Aim for 10–21°C (50–70°F).
Humidity Mist the leaves regularly.
Position Good light, but avoid exposing to direct summer sun.
Watering and feeding Water freely at all times. Feed regularly once the nutrients in the initial potting soil become depleted.
Care Deadhead regularly. Discard after flowering (although they can sometimes be kept growing into the second year, it is best to start with new plants).
Propagation Seed.

✕ Fatshedera

A bigeneric hybrid from a cross between *Fatsia japonica* and *Hedera helix* 'Hibernica'.

✕ Fatshedera lizei

Shiny, five-fingered, hand-shaped leaves. The shoots grow upwards initially, then tend to become decumbent. Rounded heads of creamy-white flowers are sometimes produced in autumn on mature plants. Will grow to 1.8m (6ft) or more if conditions are suitable, and is hardy enough to grow outside where frosts are not severe. The variegated varieties, such as 'Variegata', are slower-growing and more attractive as houseplants.

HELPFUL HINTS
Temperature Winter minimum 3°C (37°F). Keep below 21°C (70°F) if possible.
Humidity Undemanding in a cool position, mist the leaves occasionally in a warm room.
Position Good light, but avoid exposing to direct summer sun. Best possible light in winter.
Watering and feeding Water freely from spring to autumn, sparingly in winter. Feed in spring and summer.
Care Repot each spring. Provide a support if you want to grow it like an ivy, but pinch out the growing tips each spring if you prefer a more bushy plant.
Propagation Cuttings.

RIGHT: ✕ Fatshedera lizei *'Pia'*
BELOW: ✕ Fatshedera lizei *'Anne Mieke'*

Fatsia

A genus with only one species, a useful evergreen for the garden where winters are not harsh and a good houseplant for a cool and shady position.

Fatsia japonica

Deeply lobed, glossy dark green leaves, 20–40cm (8–16in) across. Variegated varieties make less vigorous and more attractive houseplants.

HELPFUL HINTS
Temperature Winter minimum 3°C (37°F), although it is not critical if the plants are exposed to a little frost. Variegated varieties are more cold-sensitive and are best in a winter minimum of about 13°C (55°F). Keep below 21°C (70°F) if possible.
Humidity Moderate humidity.
Position Good light, but not direct summer sun. Tolerates shade well.
Watering and feeding Water freely from spring to autumn, sparingly in winter. Feed in spring and summer.
Care Sponge the leaves once a month.
Propagation Cuttings; air layering; seed (for the green form).

ABOVE: Fatsia japonica

Faucaria

South African succulents with semi-cylindrical or angled fleshy leaves, and golden-yellow, daisy-like flowers in autumn.

Faucaria tigrina
Fleshy green leaves about 5cm (2in) long, speckled white and with deeply-toothed edges that create a jaw-like appearance.

HELPFUL HINTS
Temperature Winter minimum 5°C (41°F). Avoid high winter temperatures, if possible.
Humidity Tolerates dry air.
Position Brightest possible position, benefits from direct sun.
Watering and feeding Water freely in summer, sparingly in autumn and spring, and keep practically dry in winter. Feed regularly with a weak fertilizer in summer.
Care Rest the plant once the leaves begin to shrivel in autumn, and keep the compost (potting soil) and air dry

BELOW: Faucaria tigrina

to reduce the risk of rotting. Repot the plant every third year, using a cactus mixture.
Propagation Cuttings; seed.

Ferocactus

Slow-growing spherical cacti that become columnar with age. Curved, colourful spines. Specialist nurseries will offer several species, but the one described here is among those most commonly grown as houseplants.

Ferocactus latispinus
Blue-green body, spherical on small plants, with about 20 prominent ribs that bear large hooked spines. The red flowers rarely appear on specimens kept as houseplants.

HELPFUL HINTS
Temperature Winter minimum 5°C (41°F).
Humidity Tolerates dry air.
Position Brightest possible position, benefits from direct sun.
Watering and feeding Water moderately from spring to autumn. Keep practically dry in winter. Use soft water if possible.
Care Repot in spring, using a cactus mixture.
Propagation Seed; offsets.

BELOW: Ferocactus latispinus

Ficus

A huge genus with more than 800 species, most of them originating in Asia and Africa, and including the edible fig. Those used as houseplants are grown for foliage effect, and for many years *F. elastica* was one of the most popular of all houseplants. The larger species still make some of the finest focal-point plants for a room, while the trailers make useful plants for hanging pots and bottle gardens.

Ficus benghalensis
Resembles the more popular *F. elastica* but the 20cm (8in) leathery leaves are hairy. They make immense trees in the wild, and in the home will reach ceiling height after a few years if conditions are suitable.

Ficus benjamina
A tall tree with a broad crown and trailing branches in the wild, but as a pot plant the pendulous shoots give the whole plant the appearance of a small weeping tree and will seldom grow to more than 2.4m (8ft) indoors. In the species the 10cm (4in) long, pointed leaves are green, but the variegated varieties are more popular. 'Starlight' is a variety with particularly bold white markings.

Ficus deltoidea
Dark green, leathery leaves about 6–8cm (2½–3in) long, tapering towards the base and blunt at the tip. Makes a branching shrub to about 75cm (2½ft) in cultivation. May also be found under the name *F. diversifolia*.

Ficus diversifolia *see F. deltoidea.*

Ficus elastica
Large oval leaves about 30cm (1ft) long, glossy and dark green. The young leaves are sheathed in red stipules, which drop as the leaf opens. The species itself is seldom grown, and the green varieties usually sold are 'Decora' and 'Robusta', which have broader leaves, often more densely

spaced. Variegated varieties include 'Doescheri' and 'Tricolor'. 'Black Prince' has very dark foliage.

Ficus lyrata
Large, waxy leaves shaped like an upside-down violin, about 50cm (20in) long. A tall plant, usually reluctant to branch, that will reach ceiling height after a few years.

Ficus pumila
Trailing plant with thin wiry stems and heart-shaped leaves about 2.5cm (1in) long. The foliage on mature plants has thicker and longer leaves, but it is almost always seen as a houseplant with its juvenile foliage. Will also climb by means of clinging roots. 'Minima' has smaller leaves and

more compact growth. There are variegated varieties such as 'Variegata'. May also be found as *F. repens*.

Ficus radicans
Trailing, wiry stems with pointed leaves about 7.5–10cm (3–4in) long. The limp stems will trail or climb by rooting at the leaf joints. 'Variegata' has narrower leaves marked with white. More correctly known as *F. sagittata*.

Ficus religiosa
A large tree in the wild, with prop roots growing from the branches. Dull green 10–15cm (4–6in) leaves with long, slender, almost thread-like tips.

Ficus repens *see F. pumila.*

Ficus sagittata *see F. radicans.*

HELPFUL HINTS
Temperature Winter minimum 13°C (55°F).
Humidity Mist the leaves occasionally. *F. lyrata*, *F. pumila* and *F. radicans* benefit from regular misting.
Position Good light for tree and shrub types, but avoid direct summer sun through glass during the hottest part of the day. Partial shade for creeping and climbing types.
Watering and feeding Water all varieties freely from spring to autumn, but sparingly in winter. Use tepid water if possible, especially in winter. Feed in spring and summer.
Care Repot young plants every second year. Occasionally sponge the leaves of species with large, glossy foliage.
Propagation Cuttings; air layering of woody species.

LEFT: Ficus lyrata
OPPOSITE ABOVE: *Three varieties of* Ficus elastica: *'Belgica' (left), 'Robusta' (centre), 'Black Prince' (right)*
OPPOSITE BELOW: *Three varieties of* Ficus benjamina: *'Exotica' (left), 'Starlight' (centre), 'Reginald' (right)*
FAR RIGHT ABOVE: Ficus benghalensis
FAR RIGHT BELOW: Ficus deltoidea

ABOVE: Fittonia verschaffeltii

Fittonia

Non-woody, creeping ground cover plants that originate from the tropical rain forests of Peru. Although small yellowish flowers may appear in spring they are inconspicuous and the plants are grown for foliage effect.

Fittonia argyroneura *see F. verschaffeltii.*

Fittonia verschaffeltii
This species has olive green leaves about 5cm (2in) long, with deep pink veins. *F. v. argyroneura* (often sold simply as *F. argyroneura*) has pale green leaves with white veins. *F. v. argyroneura nana* (frequently sold as *F. argyroneura nana*) also has white veins on light green leaves, but these are only about 2.5cm (1in) long. Large-leaved forms grow to about 10cm (4in), the small-leaved variety only half this height.

HELPFUL HINTS
Temperature Winter minimum 16°C (60°F).
Humidity Needs high humidity.
Position Partial shade. Avoid direct sunlight.
Watering and feeding Water freely from spring to autumn, sparingly in winter. Use tepid water if possible. Feed from spring to autumn with a weak fertilizer.
Care Pinch back long, straggly shoots to keep the plant compact. Repot each

spring. Difficult to keep unless the humidity is high, but plants do well in a bottle garden.
Propagation Division; cuttings; or just pot up plants where the creeping stems have rooted.

Fuchsia

A genus of evergreen and deciduous trees and shrubs, grown mainly for their attractive pendent flowers.

Fuchsia hybrids
The hybrid fuchsias need little description as their usually bell-shaped flowers with flared 'skirts' are so well known as garden and greenhouse plants. There are single, semi-double and double varieties in a wide range of colours, but mainly pinks, reds, purples and white. The ones likely to be grown as pot plants will be hybrids, most of which will make a compact plant about 45–60cm (1½-2ft) tall. Old specimens are best discarded unless trained as a standard, when they should be repotted each spring.

HELPFUL HINTS
Temperature Aim for 10–16°C (50–60°F) in winter. Avoid high winter temperatures.
Humidity Mist the leaves occasionally when the plant has foliage.
Position Good light, but not direct summer sun.
Watering and feeding Water freely from spring to autumn while the plant is growing vigorously, sparingly early and late in the season. Water very sparingly in winter if the plants are dormant – just enough to prevent the soil drying out completely. Continue to water cuttings in leaf sufficiently to sustain growth. Feed from late spring to late summer.
Care It is natural for the leaves to fall in autumn. If possible, keep the plants in a cool, light position for the winter. New growth will appear in spring. Shorten the old shoots just before, or as, new growth starts, to keep the plant compact and bushy. The pruning can be severe as the flowers form on new growth, which is freely produced.
Propagation Cuttings.

RIGHT: Fuchsia *hybrid*

Gardenia

ABOVE: Gardenia jasminoides

Evergreen shrubs and small trees. The shrub described here is widely grown for its fragrant flowers.

G. augusta *see G. jasminoides.*

Gardenia jasminoides

Fragrant semi-double to double white flowers about 5cm (2in) across, usually borne in summer although there are varieties that flower in winter. Glossy green leaves up to 10cm (4in) long. Will make a shrub of about 1.5m (5ft) in a conservatory, but as a houseplant grows no taller than 45cm (1½ft).

HELPFUL HINTS
Temperature Winter minimum 16°C (60°F).
Humidity Mist the leaves regularly.
Position Good light, but not direct summer sun during the hottest part of the day.
Watering and feeding Water freely from spring to autumn, sparingly in winter, but never let the roots become dry. Use soft water if possible. Feed

from spring to autumn.
Care Avoid widely fluctuating temperatures when the buds are forming, as this may cause them to drop. Deadhead regularly – the blooms turn yellowish with age. After flowering the plant can be placed in a sheltered spot outside for the summer. Repot every second or third year, using an ericaceous (lime-free) compost (potting soil).
Propagation Cuttings.

Gerbera

Herbaceous perennials with daisy-like flowers. There are about 45 species but only one is grown as a pot plant.

Gerbera jamesonii

Single or double, daisy-type flowers about 5cm (2in) across, in bright colours such as red, orange, pink, yellow, and white, with a yellow centre. Main flowering time is early summer to late autumn, but they are sometimes sold

in flower in winter. Lobed hairy leaves about 15cm (6in) long arise from the base. Some grow to about 60cm (2ft) tall, but compact varieties about 25–30cm (10–12in) tall are more suitable as houseplants.

HELPFUL HINTS
Temperature Aim for 10–21°C (50–70°F) during flowering.
Humidity Mist the leaves regularly.
Position Good light, with direct sun for at least part of the day.
Watering and feeding Water freely while the plant is growing actively, more cautiously when it is resting, but never allow the roots to dry out. Feed regularly while the plant is in active growth.
Care It is difficult to keep the plant for another year when flowering has finished, unless you have a conservatory. As old plants tend to flower poorly, they are usually discarded.
Propagation Seed is the usual method, but division is an easy technique if you have an old plant.

BELOW: Gerbera jamesonii *hybrid*

Gloxinia

See Sinningia speciosa.

Guzmania

Epiphytic bromeliads, mainly from the tropical rain forests of South America. They are usually grown for their showy flower heads. The species described here is one of the most popular, but others are also sold as pot plants.

Guzmania lingulata
Rosette of foliage with strap-shaped leaves about 15–20cm (6–8in) long. The flower stalk, up to about 30cm (1ft) long, is topped by bright red or orange bracts with small yellowish-white flowers in the centre, and usual-ly blooms in summer, although commercial growers can produce plants in flower throughout the year. *G. l. minor* is a smaller plant, often only about 15cm (6in) tall.

Helpful hints
Temperature Winter minimum 16°C (60°F).
Humidity Mist occasionally in winter, regularly in summer.
Position Light shade in summer, good light in winter.
Watering and feeding Water freely from spring to autumn, sparingly in winter. Feed with a weak fertilizer in spring and summer.
Care In summer pour water into the 'vase' formed by the rosette of leaves.
Propagation Offsets; seed.

Below: Guzmania lingulata

Gymnocalycium

A genus of cacti with about 50 species. Many of them will produce their funnel-shaped flowers at an early age, but the ones most often sold are grafted forms that lack enough chlorophyll to thrive on their own roots. The grafted forms are grown for their curious appearance rather than their flowers, which tend to be less freely produced.

Gymnocalycium mihanovichii
Normally has a grey-green ribbed body with small curved thorns, and yellowish-green flowers. *G. m. friedrichii* has pink flowers. The 'curiosity' varieties have yellow, orange, red, or almost black bodies, and these are sold grafted onto a green stem from a different cactus.

ABOVE: Gymnocalycium mihanovichii

HELPFUL HINTS

Temperature Aim for a winter temperature of 5–10°C (41–50°F).
Humidity Tolerates dry air.
Position Good light, full sun in winter, but avoid direct summer sun during the hottest part of the day for coloured grafted varieties.
Watering and feeding Water moderately in summer, very sparingly at other times (just enough to prevent the body shrivelling). Feed with a weak fertilizer in summer.
Care Use a special cactus mixture if repotting.
Propagation Offsets from those species that produce them freely; coloured varieties that lack chlorophyll are best grafted.

Gynura

A genus of about 25 herbaceous or shrubby plants, from tropical areas of Asia, but only the species with attractive purple hairs are usually grown as houseplants.

Gynura aurantiaca

Dark green leaves about 15cm (6in) long, covered with purple hairs that create a velvety appearance. Upright growth to about 45–90cm (1½-3ft). Orange flowers with an unpleasant smell in winter.

Gynura procumbens *see G. sarmentosa*.

Gynura sarmentosa

Similar to previous species but smaller leaves about 7.5cm (3in) long on trailing or climbing stems. Will reach 60cm (2ft) or more with a support. May also be listed as *G. procumbens*. The plant grown as *G. sarmentosa* in cultivation is likely to be the variety *G.* 'Purple Passion'.

HELPFUL HINTS

Temperature Winter minimum 10°C (50°F).
Humidity Mist occasionally.
Position Good light, but not direct summer sun.
Watering and feeding Water freely from spring to autumn, more sparingly in winter.
Care Pinch out the growing tips periodically if you want to keep the

ABOVE: Gynura sarmentosa
BELOW: Gynura *'Purple Passion'*

plant compact and bushy. Pinch out any flowers as soon as the buds appear, as they smell unpleasant.
Propagation Cuttings.

Haworthia

A genus of clump-forming succulents with a basal rosette of warty leaves.

Haworthia fasciata
Rosette of thick, slightly incurving, finely-pointed leaves with pearly warts on the lower surface. These appear to form crosswise white bands.

Haworthia margaritifera
Similar to the previous species, but with broader rosettes, about 13cm (5in) across; the warts are arranged more randomly and do not appear to form bands.

HELPFUL HINTS
Temperature Aim for 10–13°C (50–55°F) in winter.
Humidity Tolerates dry air.
Position Brightest possible position, benefits from full sun.
Watering and feeding Water moderately from spring to autumn, very sparingly in winter. Feed with a weak fertilizer or a cactus food while plant is growing actively.
Care Repot in spring, but only when the rosette has grown too large for the pot.
Propagation Offsets; seed.

BELOW: Haworthia margaritifera

Hedera

A small genus of self-clinging climbers, but with many varieties. Plants will climb or trail, depending on how you grow them.

Hedera algeriensis *see H. canariensis.*

Hedera canariensis
Large, slightly lobed leaves, with white margins in 'Variegata', often sold under its other name of 'Gloire de Marengo'. Botanists now consider the correct name for this plant to be *H. algeriensis* 'Gloire de Marengo', but you are unlikely to find it sold under this name.

Hedera helix
This plant – the common ivy – needs no description. The leaves are much smaller than those of the previous species, and varieties are available with foliage of many different shapes and markings.

HELPFUL HINTS
Temperature Cool but frost-free is ideal, although plants are frost-hardy if suitably acclimatized. Avoid warm rooms in winter – plants are more likely to thrive in an unheated room.
Humidity Mist the leaves occasionally, regularly in summer if possible.
Position Good light or some shade.

extend the season considerably. Individual blooms are short-lived but there is a constant succession of them. Will make a shrub of 1.5m (5ft) or more given suitable conditions, but more often seen as a compact plant less than half this height indoors.

HELPFUL HINTS
Temperature Winter minimum 13°C (55°F).
Humidity Mist occasionally.
Position Good light, but not direct summer sun through glass during the hottest part of the day.
Watering and feeding Water freely from spring to autumn, sparingly in winter, but never allow the roots to dry out. Feed regularly in summer.
Care Deadhead regularly. Shorten long shoots after flowering, or in late winter. Do not turn or move the plant once buds have formed as this may cause the buds to drop. Repot each spring. The plant can be placed in a sheltered spot outdoors for the summer months.
Propagation Cuttings; seed.

BELOW: Hibiscus rosa-sinensis

OPPOSITE ABOVE: Hedera helix *'Goldchild'*
ABOVE: Hedera canariensis *'Variegata'*

Will tolerate poor light for short periods. Benefits from good light in winter, but avoid direct summer sun.
Watering and feeding Water freely in warm weather, moderately in cool temperatures. Never allow the roots to dry out. Feed regularly from spring to autumn.
Care Repot each spring unless the plant is already in a large pot. Pinch out the growing tips periodically if you want a bushy plant.
Propagation Cuttings.

Helxine

See Soleirolia.

Heptapleurum

See Schefflera.

Hibiscus

A genus that contains evergreen and deciduous trees and shrubs, herbaceous perennials, and annuals. Just one species is widely grown as a houseplant, a shrubby plant widely grown in gardens in subtropical regions.

Hibiscus rosa-sinensis
Large, double or single showy flowers about 10–13cm (4–5in) across, with stamens on a prominent central column. Colours include red, pink, orange, yellow, and white. 'Cooperi' has variegated foliage and red flowers. The main flowering time is summer, but commercial growers are able to

Hippeastrum

A genus of about 70 bulbous species from tropical and subtropical parts of America, but the plants with huge trumpet-shaped flowers grown as pot plants are hybrids. Although these are popularly known as amaryllis, this is really the botanical name of a different plant that is sometimes grown in the garden.

Hippeastrum hybrids
Clusters of three to six huge, trumpet-shaped flowers on strong stems about 60cm (2ft) tall. Colours include shades of red, pink, and white, some bicoloured. There are a few semi-double varieties. The large, strap-shaped leaves usually emerge once the flowers have started to open. It can be forced into flower in winter without the need for a period in the dark.

HELPFUL HINTS
Temperature Needs warmth to start into growth (*see* Care), but the flowers will last for longer in a cool room.
Humidity Undemanding.
Position Good light.
Watering and feeding Water moderately when the bulbs are growing, keep almost dry when resting. Feed regularly once the leaves start to grow, and cease when the resting period is due (*see* Care).
Care Bulbs prepared for early flowering should be planted when available, and they will bloom in winter. Unprepared bulbs planted at the same time will flower later. Bulbs planted in late winter or early spring will flower in mid or late spring. A soil temperature of 21°C (70°F) is required to start dormant bulbs into growth. If the roots look very dry, soak the bulbs for a few hours before potting up, burying only about half the bulb.

As soon as the flower stalk is 15–20cm (6–8in) tall, keep in a very light position. Cut off the flower stalk when blooming is over. The plant will then look unattractive and is best

ABOVE: Hippeastrum *hybrid*

placed in a conservatory or greenhouse, or outdoors for the summer once there is no risk of frost. Reduce watering in early autumn and allow the leaves to die back. Start into growth again by resuming watering a month or two later.
Propagation Offsets (which may bloom after three years); seed (unpredictable results and flowering even slower).

Howea

Evergreen palms, also occasionally seen under their old name of kentia.

Howea belmoreana
Thin green stems and arching pinnate foliage, the edges covered in woolly hairs. Will eventually grow to ceiling height indoors if conditions suit. May also be listed as *Kentia belmoreana*.

Howea forsteriana
Similar to previous species, but with broader leaflets and less arching fronds. May also be listed as *Kentia forsteriana*.

HELPFUL HINTS
Temperature Winter minimum for

RIGHT: Howea belmoreana (*syn.* Kentia belmoreana)
ABOVE RIGHT: Howea forsteriana (*syn.* Kentia forsteriana)

H. belmoreana 16°C (60°F), for *H. forsteriana* 10°C (50°F).

Humidity Mist the leaves regularly.
Position Good light, but not direct summer sun through glass during the hottest part of the day. Tolerates some shade. Good light in winter.
Watering and feeding Water moderately in summer, sparingly in winter. Keep the soil just moist. Feed in summer.
Care Sponge the leaves occasionally. The plant benefits from being stood outside in a light summer shower. Avoid using leaf shines, as some can damage the fronds.
Propagation Seed (difficult).

Hoya

Evergreen climbers, trailers, or lax shrubs, but only three out of over 200 species are grown as houseplants. The two listed are the ones most commonly grown.

Hoya bella
Fleshy leaves about 2.5cm (1in) long. Pendulous clusters of fragrant white, waxy-looking, star-shaped flowers with purplish-red centres. Flowering time is usually between late spring and early autumn. The correct botanical name for this plant is *Hoya lanceolata bella*, although you are unlikely to find it under this name.

Hoya carnosa
Similar to the previous species but with slightly larger, pale pink flowers, which are also fragrant. Leaves about 7.5cm (3in) long. There is a variegated variety.

Temperature Aim for 10–13°C (50–55°F) in winter for *H. carnosa*, and a winter minimum of 18°C (64°F) for *H. bella*.
Humidity Mist the leaves regularly, but not when plant is in bloom.
Position Good light. Some direct sun is beneficial, but avoid summer sun

ABOVE: Hoya bella

through glass during the hottest part of the day.
Watering and feeding Water freely from spring to autumn, sparingly in winter. Feed sparingly when the plant is in flower as over-feeding can inhibit flowering.
Care Provide suitable support if the plant is to be grown as a climber. A trellis or moss pole is suitable, but *H. bella* can also be grown in a hanging basket. Do not move the plant once flower buds form. Do not repot until absolutely necessary as root disturbance is resented.
Propagation Semi-ripe tip cuttings or eye cuttings. *H. bella* is sometimes grafted onto *H. carnosa*.

Hyacinthus

A small genus of bulbous plants, from Asia Minor and around the Mediterranean. Only one is widely grown, but its varieties are among the most popular indoor bulbs for winter colour and fragrance.

Hyacinthus orientalis
The dense spikes of the hyacinth need no description. There are many varieties in shades of red, pink, mauve, blue, yellow, and white. Multiflora varieties produce several small spikes from each bulb instead of one large one. Flowering time ranges from early winter to mid spring, depending on variety, planting time, and

whether the bulb has been specially prepared for early flowering. Consult a bulb catalogue for specific varieties, planting and flowering times.

Temperature Hardy. Keep as cool as possible unless advancing flowering, and then only force once the bud has emerged. Once in bloom, the cooler the room, the longer the flowers will last.
Humidity Undemanding.
Position Good light once flower buds start to show colour. Once in full flower, can be positioned anywhere as a short-term houseplant.
Watering and feeding Ensure the roots do not dry out at any time. Feeding is not necessary unless you want to save the bulbs to plant in the garden.
Care Hyacinths should be regarded as short-term houseplants. If you want to plant the bulbs in the garden after flowering, continue to water and feed regularly until the leaves begin to die down. At this stage, place in a garden frame to acclimatize to outside conditions and then plant in the garden. Do not use again indoors.
Propagation Offset bulbs can be grown on, but this is not practical for propagating houseplants. Buy fresh bulbs each year.

BELOW: Hyacinthus orientalis *variety*

Hydrangea

A genus of over 20 deciduous shrubs and deciduous and evergreen climbers, but only the species below is used as a pot plant.

Hydrangea macrophylla

Shrub with broad oval, coarsely toothed deciduous leaves about 15cm (6in) long, and ball-shaped flower heads in shades of blue, pink, and white. Mophead varieties have rounded heads of flowers that all look the same; Lacecap varieties have an outer ring of open flowers. Although they make shrubs of at least 1.5m (5ft) in the garden, these plants are only used indoors while small. Hydrangeas are usually sold as flowering pot plants in flower in spring, but specially-treated plants may be available in bloom at other times of year.

HELPFUL HINTS

Temperature Frost-hardy, but indoors these plants are best in a winter minimum of 7°C (45°F). Move them to a warm, bright position in mid winter, when you can increase watering. If possible, avoid a very warm room.

Humidity Mist occasionally.

Position Good light or light shade. Some direct sun is beneficial in winter but avoid hot summer sun.

Watering and feeding Water freely from spring to autumn, sparingly in early winter. Use soft water if possible. Feed regularly while plants are growing actively.

Care Flower colour can be affected by the acidity of the compost (potting soil). Use an ericaceous (acidic, humusy, lime-free) mixture if you want blue flowers. You can also buy proprietary blueing compounds but plants must be treated before they flower. Never allow the roots to dry out during the growing season. Cut back the stems to half their height after flowering. The plants are not particularly attractive when flowering has finished, so stand in the garden for the summer.

Propagation Semi-ripe cuttings.

BELOW: Hydrangea macrophylla

ABOVE: Hymenocallis × festalis

Hymenocallis

A genus of about 40 bulbous plants, only a few of which are sometimes grown as pot plants. You can buy the bulbs from specialist bulb suppliers.

Hymenocallis × festalis

Large white central cup surrounded by backward-curving petals, in late spring or summer. Fragrant. Strap-shaped leaves die down in autumn. A hybrid between *H. narcissiflora* and *H. longipetala*.

Hymenocallis narcissiflora

Clusters of three to six pendulous white flowers with a white funnel-shaped fringed cup surrounded by backward-curving slender petals. Fragrant. Leaves die down in autumn.

HELPFUL HINTS

Temperature Winter minimum 15°C (59°F), although the plant may be dormant for most of that time.

Humidity Undemanding.

Position Good light, but avoid direct summer sun through glass during the hottest part of the day.

Watering and feeding Water freely during the growing season. Keep the species that die back practically dry in winter and water those that retain their foliage cautiously. Feed regularly when active growth starts.

Care More likely to be available as dry bulbs than growing plants. Start the bulbs into growth in late winter or early spring.

Propagation Offsets.

Hypocyrta

A small genus of about nine species, which has since been divided by botanists into other varieties. Only one of these is widely grown.

Hypocyrta glabra

Shiny dark green, leathery leaves, about 3cm (1¼in) long on compact plants 15–23cm (6–9in) tall. Small orange, waxy-looking flowers appear along the stems in summer. Now considered by botanists to be more correctly *Nematanthus*, although you are much more likely to find it sold under the name used here.

BELOW: Hypocyrta glabra

HELPFUL HINTS

Temperature Winter minimum 10°C (50°F).

Humidity Mist the leaves regularly.

Position Good light, but do not expose to direct summer sun during the hottest part of the day. Best possible light in winter.

Watering and feeding Water moderately from spring to autumn, sparingly in winter.

Care Cut back after flowering, shortening the shoots by about a third. Avoid high winter temperatures as the plant benefits from a rest at this time.

Propagation Cuttings; division; seed.

Hypoestes

A genus of mainly evergreen perennials and sub-shrubs, only two of which are grown as houseplants. The one described here is the species most commonly seen.

Hypoestes phyllostachya

Pointed, oval leaves about 6cm (2½in)

ABOVE: Hypoestes phyllostachya (*syn.* H. sanguinolenta)

long, covered with red or pink spots and blotches. The intensity of variegation depends on variety and growing conditions: some appear mainly pink, red or white, with areas of green, others are mainly green with more distinct spots of pink or white. Colouring is usually more vivid with some direct sunlight. Can be kept to 30–60cm (1–2ft) by regular pruning. Also sold as *H. sanguinolenta*, although strictly this is a different plant.

Hypoestes sanguinolenta *see* H. *phyllostachya*.

HELPFUL HINTS

Temperature Winter minimum 13°C (55°F).

Humidity Mist the leaves regularly.

Position Good light, but avoid direct summer sun through glass during the hottest part of the day.

Watering and feeding Water freely from spring to autumn, sparingly in winter. Feed regularly in summer. Over-feeding may encourage tall, spindly growth.

Care Pinch out the growing tips and cut back straggly shoots from time to time to keep the plant compact. If it becomes tall and straggly, cut it back – shoots will regrow from near the base. Pinch out flowers as they will spoil the plant's compact shape.

Propagation Cuttings; seed.

Impatiens

A large genus of about 850 species, but those used as houseplants are mainly derived from the single species *I. walleriana*. These plants have been subject to intensive breeding; apart from compact and floriferous varieties (used for summer bedding as well as pot plants), foliage plants such as the New Guinea hybrids have extended the range of impatiens that are suitable for the home.

Impatiens hybrids

Masses of spurred, flat flowers, 2.5–5cm (1–2in) across, at any time of the year if the temperature can be maintained above 16°C (60°F). Blooms are mostly in shades of red, orange, pink, and white, of which many are multicoloured and some double. Small pale green leaves on brittle stems. The New Guinea hybrids have large, more lance-shaped, bronze or variegated leaves and generally make taller plants, of 30–60cm (1–2ft). The blooms on New Guinea hybrids are usually fewer but larger.

Helpful Hints

Temperature Winter minimum 13°C (55°F); 16°C (60°F) if you want to keep plants flowering.
Humidity Mist the leaves occasionally, but try to keep water away from the flowers.
Position Good light, but not direct summer sun during the hottest part of the day. Will tolerate shade, but the plants will be taller and lankier and the blooms less prolific.
Watering and feeding Water freely from spring to autumn, sparingly in winter.
Care If an old plant has become tall and lanky, cut it back to within a few inches of the base – it will usually regrow. Repot old plants in spring if necessary. As impatiens are so easy to grow from cuttings and seed, however, it is generally preferable to raise new plants regularly and to discard old ones.

TOP: Impatiens *hybrid*
ABOVE: Impatiens, *a New Guinea hybrid*

Propagation Seed; cuttings. Most New Guinea hybrids can only be raised from cuttings, although a few varieties can be grown from seed.

Iresine

A genus of evergreen perennials grown for their colourful foliage, widely used as formal bedding in countries where frosts do not occur.

Iresine herbstii

Spatula-shaped leaves about 7.5cm (3in) long, dark reddish-brown with carmine veins. 'Aureoreticulata' has green leaves with yellow veins, on red stems. Grows to about 60cm (2ft), but is kept smaller by pruning.

Iresine lindenii

Narrow, glossy deep red leaves with prominent veins. Uncommon.

Helpful Hints

Temperature Winter minimum 13°C (55°F).
Humidity Mist the leaves regularly.
Position Good light, but not direct summer sun through glass during the hottest part of the day.

Watering and feeding Water freely from spring to autumn, sparingly in winter. Feed from spring to autumn.
Care Pinch out the growing tips occasionally to encourage compact and bushy growth. Will tolerate regular clipping if necessary. Can be stood outdoors for the summer. Overwintered plants often look unhappy by spring, but cuttings root easily and it may be more practical to start again with new plants.
Propagation Cuttings.

BELOW: Iresine lindenii

Iris

A large group of plants that includes hardy border plants with rhizomes and some that form bulbs. Those sometimes used as short-term houseplants are hardy dwarf bulbous species useful for providing spring colour indoors.

Iris danfordiae
Fragrant yellow flowers on stems about 10cm (4in) tall appear before the leaves. The grass-like foliage grows to twice this height, but plants are normally placed outside before the foliage becomes obtrusive.

Iris reticulata hybrids
Slightly fragrant blue or purple flowers (depending on variety) with yellow markings. About 15cm (6in) tall in flower, although the grass-like foliage later grows taller.

HELPFUL HINTS
Temperature Frost-hardy. Keep cool to prolong flower life.
Humidity Undemanding.
Position Good light once the buds begin to open.

RIGHT: Iris reticulata 'Harmony'
BELOW: Iris danfordiae

Watering and feeding Keep the potting mixture moist but not wet.
Care Plant the bulbs in early or mid autumn, in pots or bowls, and place outside or in a garden frame. Once the shoots are through bring the bulbs indoors and keep in a light place. Discard or plant out in the garden once flowering is over. Do not reuse the bulbs indoors.
Propagation Offsets, but for growing in pots or bowls it is best to buy fresh bulbs each year.

Jasminum

A genus of about 200 species, mainly deciduous and evergreen woody climbers. Being vigorous climbers, they are more suitable for a conservatory than a living-room, especially if you want to keep them as long-term plants.

Jasminum officinale
Deciduous climber with divided leaves and loose sprays of fragrant white flowers about 2.5cm (1in) across in summer. 'Grandiflorum' (which may also be seen as *J. o. affine*), with larger flowers tinged pink on the outside, is a form commonly sold. Can be grown outdoors where winters are mild.

Jasminum polyanthum
Similar to the previous species, but usually pink in bud, with plumes of

ABOVE: Jasminum polyanthum

fragrant white flowers in winter.

HELPFUL HINTS
Temperature Winter minimum 7°C (45°F).
Humidity Mist the leaves regularly.
Position Good light with some direct sun.
Watering and feeding Water freely from spring to autumn, but in winter keep compost (potting soil) only moist enough to prevent it from completely drying out. Feed regularly during periods of active growth.
Care Grow in a large pot with a suitable support. Prune back to contain size if necessary – jasminums will soon reach 3m (10ft) or more if left to grow unchecked. Avoid high winter temperatures. Can be stood outside in summer.
Propagation Cuttings.

Justicia

Genus of evergreen perennials, shrubs and sub-shrubs, from tropical and subtropical regions, but only the species described here is widely grown as a pot plant. You are just as likely to find it sold under its other name of *Beloperone guttata*.

Justicia brandegeana
Small white flowers surrounded by reddish-brown bracts that overlap like roof tiles. These bracts are the main reason for growing the plant, as they

Kalanchoe

A genus of about 125 perennial succulents or shrubs with fleshy leaves, which includes a number of popular and undemanding houseplants.

Kalanchoe blossfeldiana hybrids
Small, leathery, serrated oval leaves, which often turn reddish in strong sunlight. Clusters of long-lasting, short-stalked small flowers in shades of red, orange, yellow, and lilac. Although naturally spring-flowering plants, commercial growers are able to produce flowering specimens throughout the year.

Only hybrids are grown, and most of these make compact plants 15–30cm (6–12in) tall. There are also miniatures.

Although there are many named varieties, they are usually sold simply by colour.

Kalanchoe daigremontiana *see Bryophyllum daigremontianum.*

Kalanchoe manginii
Lance- or spatula-shaped leaves about 2.5cm (1in) long, on upright stems that gradually arch over. Larger, pendent, bell-like orange-red flowers in arching sprays.

Kalanchoe tubiflora *see Bryophyllum tubiflorum.*

remain attractive for a long period. The plants can be bought in flower every month of the year. Old plants can reach 90cm (3ft) or more, but in the home they tend to be discarded before they reach this size and are usually only half this height.

HELPFUL HINTS
Temperature Aim for 10–16°C (50–60°F) in winter.
Humidity Mist occasionally.
Position Good light, including some

LEFT: Justicia brandegeana

direct sun, but not direct summer sun through glass during the hottest part of the day.
Watering and feeding Water freely from spring to autumn, sparingly in winter. Feed regularly from spring to autumn.
Care Repot each spring. At the same time, prune the shoots back by one-third to half to keep the plant a compact shape.
Propagation Cuttings.

ABOVE: Kalanchoe blossfeldiana *hybrid*
RIGHT: Kalanchoe manginii

HELPFUL HINTS
Temperature Winter minimum 10°C (50°F).
Humidity Tolerates dry air.
Position Good light, including some direct sun, but avoid direct summer sun through glass during the hottest part of the day.
Watering and feeding Water freely from spring to autumn, sparingly in

winter. Feed regularly from spring to autumn.
Care Repot after flowering if saving an old plant, and shorten the shoots to keep growth compact. As they are easy to raise and cheap to buy, however, most people treat them as annuals and discard them when flowering is over. If raising your own plants they will only develop flower buds when

day length is less than 12 hours. It is possible to adjust flowering time by artificially controlling daylight hours.
Propagation Cuttings; seed.

Kentia

See Howea.

Lilium

A genus of bulbous plants widely grown in gardens. Most species, especially those chosen as pot plants, are hybrids. They have become more popular as commercially grown house-plants with the introduction of compact varieties and new techniques with growth regulators to keep the plants dwarf. Apart from the hybrids, species such as *L. auratum, L. longiflorum, L. regale,* and *L. speciosum* are sometimes grown in pots.

Lilium hybrids
Most hybrids have trumpet-shaped or backward-curving petals, in shades of red, orange, yellow, and white, usually spotted, mottled, or flushed with another colour. There are hundreds of varieties, with new ones introduced annually. Consult a good bulb catalogue for the most appropriate varieties to grow in pots, and choose the most compact ones for the home. You may find it difficult to keep home-grown plants as compact as those produced by nurseries: special facilities and chemicals are used to produce small plants in full bloom.

HELPFUL HINTS
Temperature Aim for 3-10°C (37-50°F). Avoid high temperatures.
Humidity Mist occasionally.
Position Good light, but avoid exposing to direct summer sun.
Watering and feeding Keep the compost (potting soil) moist during the period of active growth, and feed regularly.
Care Bulbs are usually planted in autumn or mid to late winter, according to when they are available. Pot up large ones singly, smaller ones three to a pot. There should be at least 5cm (2in) of compost (potting soil) beneath the bulb and about 10cm (4in) above, but lilies vary in the way they form roots, so be guided by any instructions that come with the bulb or

LEFT: Lilium *hybrid*

in the catalogue. Keep the planted bulbs in a cool place, such as a garden frame, cellar or basement, with the soil just moist. Ensure there is good light once shoots appear, and keep at the recommended temperature once buds can be seen. When the buds show colour the pots can be moved to a warmer room, but avoid high temperatures that will shorten the life of the blooms. Plant in the garden after flowering.

Propagation Offsets or scales, but this is a slow job requiring an area where they can be grown on. Buy new bulbs each time for use indoors.

Lisianthus russellianus

See Eustoma grandiflora.

Lithops

Prostrate succulents with pairs of fused swollen leaves, which eventually grow into small clumps. They are interesting plants that mimic stones or pebbles, but are slow-growing. Many species are available but the one described below is typical of those you are likely to find.

BELOW: Lithops bella

Lithops bella
Pairs of pale brownish-yellow, fused leaves with slightly depressed darker patches. White daisy-like flowers in late summer or early autumn. About 2.5cm (1in) high.

HELPFUL HINTS
Temperature Winter minimum 7°C (45°F).
Humidity Tolerates dry air.
Position Good light with plenty of sun. Tolerates full summer sun.
Watering and feeding Water carefully at all times, only moderately in summer and not at all in winter. Start watering again when the old leaves split to reveal the new ones beneath. Feeding is seldom necessary, but if the plants have been in the same pot for many years, feed occasionally with a cactus fertilizer.
Care Repot only when the pot has become filled with leaves. Lithops look attractive if grown in a landscaped container with the surface decorated with gravel or pebbles to blend in with the plants.
Propagation Seed.

Lobivia

A genus of spherical to columnar cacti, forming clumps with age. Lobivias flower at an early age.

Lobivia densispina
Densely thorned, short-cylindrical body, sometimes branched. Wide, funnel-shaped, flowers. More correctly named *Echinopsis kuehnrichii*.

Lobivia famatimensis
Cylindrical body with about 20 ribs and yellowish thorns. The flowers appear in early summer, but are short-lived. More correctly named *Rebutia famatimensis*.

Lobivia hertrichiana
Spherical body with 11 notched ribs covered with yellow thorns. Red, short-lived flowers in early summer.

TOP: Lobivia densispina
ABOVE: Lobivia hertrichiana

HELPFUL HINTS
Temperature Aim for 5-7°C (41-45°F) in winter. Avoid high winter temperatures, but keep frost-free.
Humidity Tolerates dry air.
Position Best possible light, including some direct sun.
Watering and feeding Water moderately in summer, sparingly from autumn to spring. Keep practically dry in winter. Use soft water if possible. Feed with a weak fertilizer in summer.
Care Pay special attention to winter temperatures to encourage the plant to flower well. Repot young plants each spring.
Propagation Offsets (unrooted ones can be used as cuttings); seed.

Lytocaryum

See Cocos.

Mammillaria

A genus of about 150 hemispherical, spherical, or columnar cacti, most of which are compact in growth and free-flowering. Cacti specialists offer a wide range of species, and those described here are only a selection of those available.

Mammillaria bocasana
Spherical or cylindrical, maturing to form a clump, covered with hooked thorns and white hairs. Reddish flowers that are white inside.

Mammillaria elongata
Clump-forming with columnar stems, densely covered with yellow to brown spines. Cream flowers in summer.

Mammillaria wildii
Clump-forming, branching columnar stems with white thorns and long hairs. Rings of small white flowers appear in spring.

Mammillaria zeilmanniana
Clusters of short, cylindrical stems, with dense covering of hooked spines.

Bell-shaped flowers, deep purple to pink, sometimes white in spring.

HELPFUL HINTS
Temperature Winter minimum 7°C (45°F).
Humidity Tolerates dry air.
Position Best possible light, with some sun.
Watering and feeding Water moderately from spring to autumn, but keep almost dry in winter.
Care Repot young plants annually in spring; older ones will not require such frequent repotting.
Propagation Cuttings; seed.

ABOVE: Mammillaria zeilmanniana
BELOW: Mammillaria bocasana *(left) and* M. wildii *(right)*

TOP: Maranta leuconeura erythroneura (*syn.* 'Erythrophylla' *and* M. tricolor)
ABOVE: Maranta leuconeura kerchoveana

Maranta

A small genus of tropical plants from regions of Central and South America, grown for their attractive foliage.

Maranta bicolor
Round to oval leaves up to 15cm (6in) long, with five to eight brown blotches on either side of the main vein and purple undersides. Small white flowers are sometimes produced.

Maranta leuconeura
A tuberous plant with slightly smaller leaves than the previous species. Varieties of this species most commonly grown include *M. l. erythroneura* (syn. 'Erythrophylla', sometimes sold

as *M. tricolor*), which has prominent red veins and yellow markings near main vein, and *M. l. kerchoveana*, with brown blotches turning green with age.

HELPFUL HINTS
Temperature Winter minimum 10°C (50°F).
Humidity Needs high humidity. Mist the leaves regularly.
Position Good light, but avoid exposing to direct summer sun. Best possible light in winter.
Watering and feeding Water freely from spring to autumn, sparingly in winter. Use soft water if possible. Feed regularly in summer.
Care Repot every second spring.
Propagation Division.

Microcoelum

See Cocos.

Mimosa

A large genus of shrubs, trees, climbers and annuals, including plants with very varied characteristics and requirements, but the one most likely to be grown as a houseplant is the species described here.

Mimosa pudica
Feathery-looking leaves with leaflets, which are highly responsive to being touched. First the leaflets fold, then the whole leaf droops (at night they fold naturally). After about a half to one hour the leaves resume their original position. Small flowers like pink balls are produced in summer. Although a short-lived shrub, it is usually treated as an annual, when it seldom exceeds 60cm (2ft).

HELPFUL HINTS
Temperature Winter minimum 16°C (60°F).
Humidity Mist the leaves regularly.
Position Good light with some direct sun, but avoid direct summer sun during the hottest part of the day.
Watering and feeding Water freely from spring to autumn, sparingly in summer. Use soft water if possible. Feed regularly in summer.
Care Repot in spring, but as plants are easily raised from seed, they are best treated as annuals.
Propagation Seed; cuttings.

BELOW: Mimosa pudica

ABOVE: Monstera deliciosa

Monstera

Woody climbers, most growing as epiphytes, from tropical regions of America.

Monstera deliciosa
Climber with thick stems and aerial roots by which it clings. The large leaves, up to 60cm (2ft) across, are entire and heart-shaped initially, but become incised and perforated with age. There is also a variegated variety. White lily-like flowers sometimes appear, but usually only on plants grown in a greenhouse or conservatory. Will easily grow to ceiling height. May be found under its old name of *Philodendron pertusum*.

HELPFUL HINTS
Temperature Winter minimum 10°C (50°F).
Humidity Mist the leaves regularly.
Position Good light or shade, out of direct sunlight.
Watering and feeding Water freely from spring to autumn, sparingly in winter.
Routine care Provide a suitable climbing support, such as a moss-covered pole. Lightly sponge the leaves occasionally.
Propagation Cuttings; air layering.

Nematanthus

See Hypocyrta.

Narcissus

A genus of well-known bulbous plants that includes the popular daffodil. Suitable varieties can be grown in pots for early flowering indoors.

Narcissus hybrids
There are hundreds of varieties, ranging from traditional trumpet daffodils to miniatures, mainly in the usual shades of yellow or white. Consult a bulb catalogue for varieties suitable for forcing in pots. 'Paperwhite' (white with yellow eye, fragrant) and 'Soleil d'Or' (yellow, with deep yellow centre) are sold primarily for indoor use.

HELPFUL HINTS
Temperature Aim for 15–21°C (59–70°F) for the varieties mentioned above. Garden varieties being used in the home should be kept cool until the flower buds have emerged from the bulb (*see* Care), then brought into warmth.
Humidity Undemanding.
Position The varieties mentioned above should be kept in good light all the time. Normal varieties should be in good light when the buds have emerged, but may be placed anywhere once in flower as they are short-term houseplants.
Watering and feeding Water moderately while the bulbs are growing. If keeping the bulbs to grow in the garden, continue watering until planted out. Feeding is unnecessary.
Care The two varieties mentioned specifically can be grown in pots, but are sometimes grown in bowls of water, supported by pebbles or marbles (keep base of bulb above the water). These are kept indoors, and will flower very early. Garden varieties forced in pots should be potted up then kept in a cool, dark place until rooted – aim for 7–10°C (45–50°F) at this

ABOVE: Narcissus *'Cheerfulness'*

stage. Bring indoors or into the warmth only when the flower buds have clearly emerged from the bulbs.
Propagation Offsets and scales (bulb-cuttings), but this is impractical in the home. Buy fresh bulbs each year.

Neanthe

See Chamaedorea.

Neoregelia

Rosette-forming epiphytic bromeliads, mainly from Brazil.

Neoregelia carolinae
Leaves about 40cm (16in) long and 5cm (2in) wide form a broad rosette, normally green but those that surround the top of the 'vase' created by the rosette are flushed red when the plant is in flower (usually in summer). *N. c. tricolor* has slightly narrower leaves streaked yellow along their length. The purple-blue flowers nestle in the water-filled 'vase'.

HELPFUL HINTS
Temperature Winter minimum 13°C (55°F).
Humidity Mist the leaves regularly.
Position Good light, but avoid exposing to direct sun.

BELOW: Neoregelia carolinae

Watering and feeding Water the compost (potting mixture) moderately at all times, but keep the 'vase' topped up with water. Use soft water if possible. Use a weak fertilizer (add it to the soil or 'vase') in summer.
Care The plant will die after flowering, so once in bloom it does not matter much where you place it. But if you want to propagate new plants from the offsets produced from around the parent, continue to feed and grow in good light. These are not easy plants to keep long-term in the home. It is best to grow them to flowering stage in a greenhouse or conservatory, bringing them indoors only when they begin to show colour.
Propagation Offsets.

Nephrolepis

Genus of about 30 terrestrial and epiphytic, evergreen or semi-evergreen ferns, distributed over tropical regions in all parts of the world. The species below is the only one widely grown as a pot plant.

Nephrolepis exaltata
Pinnate leaves about 45–60cm (1½–2ft) long, forming a dense clump. There are variations on the basic plant, including 'Bostoniensis', with more gracefully drooping leaves than the true species, 'Teddy Junior', with

crimped and undulating leaflets, and 'Whitmanii', with deeply incised, lacy-looking leaflets.

HELPFUL HINTS
Temperature Winter minimum 18°C (64°F).
Humidity Mist the leaves regularly.
Position Good light, but not direct sun.
Watering and feeding Water freely in summer, cautiously in winter, but with care at all times. The plant is vulnerable to over- and under-watering, so try to keep the roots moist without being wet. Use soft water if possible.
Care Repot in spring if the plant becomes too large for its pot, but do not be surprised if the plant deteriorates before this stage is reached – it is difficult to keep in good condition in the home. Provide a position away from draughts.
Propagation Plantlets, which develop at intervals along the rhizomes. Spores can be used only for the species, and not the varieties.

Nerium

A genus of evergreen shrubs grown for their flowers. The species described here is widely grown as a pot plant, and is a very popular outdoor shrub in southern Europe and America.

ABOVE: Nerium oleander

Nerium oleander
Leathery, willow-like leaves 15–20cm (6–8in) long, arranged around the stem in groups of three. Clusters of white, red, pink, or lilac flowers. There are many varieties, including those with double blooms. Will make a large shrub of 1.8m (6ft) or more in suitable conditions, and, when fully grown, is more suitable for a conservatory than the home.

HELPFUL HINTS
Temperature Winter minimum 7°C (45°F).
Humidity Undemanding.
Position Good light, with some direct sun.
Watering and feeding Water freely spring to autumn, cautiously in winter; do not allow roots to become dry. Feed regularly in spring and summer.
Care The plant can be stood outdoors, perhaps on the patio, for the summer. Acclimatize it gradually, and bring in before the nights become cold. In autumn, shorten stems that have flowered by about half to keep the plant compact and encourage bushiness.
Propagation Cuttings.

LEFT: Nephrolepis exaltata *'Bostoniensis'*

Nertera

A small genus of creeping perennials grown for their bead-like berries. Only one species is cultivated.

Nertera depressa *see N. granadensis.*

Nertera granadensis
Mound-forming plant with creeping stems and small rounded leaves about 6mm (¼in) long. Tiny greenish-white flowers in spring followed by bright orange berries in autumn. You may find it sold under its other name of *N. depressa.*

HELPFUL HINTS
Temperature Winter minimum 7°C (45°F).
Humidity Mist the leaves occasionally.
Position Good light, with some direct sun.
Watering and feeding Water freely from spring to autumn, sparingly in winter. Never allow the roots to dry out completely.
Care The plant is unattactive until the berries appear, but you can stand it outdoors from early summer until the berries form. The plants are usually bought when in fruit and discarded afterwards, but they can be overwintered with care.
Propagation Division; seed.

BELOW: Nertera granadensis

Nidularium

Rosette-forming epiphytic bromeliads, similar to neoregelias.

Nidularium billbergioides citrinum
A rosette of arching strap-shaped leaves, to about 45–60cm (1½–2ft). The true flowers are white and inconspicuous, but the head of yellow bracts is bright and long-lasting.

Nidularium fulgens
Spreading rosettes of broad, strap-shaped, spiny-toothed leaves. Tubular white and purple flowers nestle in the 'vase' formed by the rosette of foliage, mainly in summer. When the plant is flowering the bright red bracts surrounding the 'vase' are the plant's main feature.

Nidularium innocentii
Similar to the previous species, but the undersides of the leaves are purple and the flowers white. The bracts also colour well at flowering.

LEFT BELOW: Nidularium innocentii striatum
LEFT ABOVE: Nidularium fulgens
ABOVE: Nidularium billbergiodes citrinum

HELPFUL HINTS

Temperature Winter minimum 10°C (50°F).
Humidity Mist occasionally.
Position Good light, but not direct sun.
Watering and feeding Water freely from spring to autumn, sparingly in winter. Keep the 'vase' topped up with water from spring to autumn. Feed with a weak fertilizer in summer.
Care The parent plant will die after flowering, and young plants propagated from offsets take a few years to make attractive specimens. If you do not have a greenhouse or conservatory where you can grow them on, it may be best to buy plants in flower and discard them afterwards.
Propagation Offsets.

Notocactus

A small genus of mainly spherical cacti, often ribbed and densely spiny, that flower young and prolifically.

Notocactus apricus
A small species forming a flattened and much-ribbed sphere. Very spiny. Yellow flowers about 7.5cm (3in) across in summer. Now also known as *Parodia concinna*.

Notocactus ottonis
A ribbed spherical body with stiff spines. Golden yellow flowers about 7.5cm (3in) across in summer. Now also known as *Parodia ottonis*.

HELPFUL HINTS

Temperature Winter minimum 10°C (50°F).
Humidity Tolerates dry air.
Position Good light but only limited direct sun. Provide shade from bright direct sun in spring; in summer a mixture of sun and some shade.

TOP: Notocactus apricus
ABOVE: Notocactus ottonis

Watering and feeding Water freely from spring to autumn, more sparingly in winter.
Care Generally trouble-free, but do not keep too warm in winter.
Propagation Seed; cuttings in species that produce offsets.

Odontoglossum

Epiphytic orchids from the mountain forests of tropical America. The species below is often particularly successful in a living-room, others can be more demanding in the home.

Odontoglossum grande
Large brown, yellow, and white flowers, up to 15cm (6in) across, produced in autumn. There are a number of varieties of this species. Now considered to be more correctly named *Rossioglossum grande*.

HELPFUL HINTS
Temperature Winter minimum 13°C (55°F).

Humidity Mist occasionally.
Position Good light, but not direct summer sun. Best possible light in winter.
Watering and feeding Water freely from spring to autumn, and very sparingly in winter (just enough to prevent the pseudobulbs from shrivelling). Use soft water if possible. Feed with a weak fertilizer from spring to autumn.
Care Use a special orchid compost (potting soil) when repotting. This becomes necessary when growth begins to wilt and die back.
Propagation Division.

BELOW: Odontoglossum grande
RIGHT BELOW: Opuntia microdasys

Opuntia

A large genus of more than 200 cacti, ranging from low ground-cover to tree-sized plants. Many of these are popular with collectors.

Opuntia cylindrica
Cylindrical stems which become branching with age. Older plants – usually those over 1.8m (6ft) tall – produce saucer-shaped, reddish-pink flowers in spring or early summer.

Opuntia microdasys
Flat, pale green pads, usually growing to about 30cm (1ft) as a houseplant, with tufts of tiny hooked barbs known as glochids. There are several varieties, and in *O. m. albinospina* the glochids are white. Flowers are usually yellow, about 5cm (2in) across, but only produced on larger plants than are usually found in the home.

Opuntia phaeacantha
Oval to round pads up to 15cm (6in) long, with brownish-yellow glochids. Yellow flowers. Cold tolerant.

Opuntia vestita
Cylindrical joints, the sections easily

ABOVE: Opuntia vestita *(left)*, O. cylindrica *(centre)*, O. phaeacantha *(right)*

broken off, with conspicuous wool and long hairs. Small, deep red flowers.

HELPFUL HINTS
Temperature Winter minimum 7°C (45°F).
Humidity Tolerates dry air.
Position Good light. Benefits from direct sun.
Watering and feeding Water moderately from spring to autumn, very sparingly in winter. Feed with a weak fertilizer, or one formulated for cacti, in summer.
Care Repot in spring if necessary – those with flat pads usually do well in an ordinary loam-based compost (potting soil), others prefer a cactus mixture. Avoid warm temperatures in winter. Some species can be grown outdoors if frosts are not severe.
Propagation Cuttings (detach pads from species'that have them); seed.

Oxalis

A large genus of tuberous-, rhizomatous-, and fibrous-rooted perennials, most combining attractive foliage with pretty flowers. Some species are troublesome as garden weeds.

Oxalis deppei
A clover-like plant with four green leaflets blotched pinkish-brown at the base. Red or purplish-violet small, funnel-shaped flowers in late spring or summer. Frost-hardy. Is now considered by botanists to be more correctly named *O. tetraphylla*, but is still widely sold under the name given here.

Oxalis tetraphylla *see O. deppei*.

HELPFUL HINTS
Temperature Winter minimum 7°C (45°F). Some species are hardy, but indoors they are best kept at the minimum suggested.
Humidity Undemanding.
Position Good light or partial shade, out of direct summer sun.
Watering and feeding Water freely while in active growth. Feed regularly during the growing season.
Care Avoid high temperatures – otherwise the plant will be short-lived. Plants are sometimes sold for winter decoration indoors, but hardy species are best planted in the garden when flowering has finished.
Propagation Offsets.

BELOW: Oxalis deppei

Pachystachys

A genus of evergreen perennials and shrubs, with only one species being grown as a houseplant.

Pachystachys lutea
Cone-shaped yellow flower heads, about 10cm (4in) long, over a period from late spring to autumn. The true flowers are white and protrude from the longer-lasting yellow bracts. Pointed oval leaves.

HELPFUL HINTS
Temperature Winter minimum 13°C (55°F).
Humidity Mist the leaves regularly in summer.
Position Good light, but not direct summer sun during the hottest part of the day.
Watering and feeding Water freely from spring to autumn, sparingly in winter. Feed regularly in summer.
Care Cut off the flower heads when flowering is over, and shorten long shoots in spring to keep the plant compact. Repot annually in spring.
Propagation Cuttings.

BELOW: Pachystachys lutea

Paphiopedilum

A genus of about 60 orchids, but it is the hybrids that are usually grown.

Paphiopedilum hybrids
Striking flowers, about 5–10cm (2–4in) across, with a lower lip that forms a pouch, and wing-like petals. Colours vary according to variety but are usually in shades of brown, orange, amber, green, and purple, often heavily streaked or spotted. Most bloom in winter or spring. You may sometimes find paphiopedilums sold under their old name of cypripedium.

HELPFUL HINTS
Temperature Winter minimum 13°C (55°F).
Humidity Mist occasionally.
Position Good light, but avoid exposing to direct sun.
Watering and feeding Water freely from spring to autumn, sparingly in winter. Use soft water if possible. Feed with a weak fertilizer while growing actively.
Care Remove any old and yellowing leaves periodically and keep a watch for slugs, which may spoil the foliage.
Propagation Division.

RIGHT: Paphiopedilum *'Green Gable'*

Parodia

Rounded cacti, some becoming cylindrical with age, with ribs and usually thorns. You may find that some plants have been grafted.

Parodia aureispina
A spherical body up to about 10cm (4in) across, with many conspicuous white and yellow thorns. Yellow flowers about 2.5cm (1in) across in spring.

Parodia chrysacanthion
A spherical body up to about 10cm (4in) across, sometimes flattened with age, with bristle-like spines. Yellow flowers in spring.

HELPFUL HINTS

Temperature Aim for 7–12°C (45–53°F) in winter.

Humidity Tolerates dry air.

Position Best possible light. Benefits from full sun.

Watering and feeding Water moderately from spring to autumn, keep practically dry in winter. Use soft water if possible. Feed in summer with a weak fertilizer or cactus food.

Care Plants are slow-growing, but if they need repotting use a special cactus mixture if possible.

Propagation Seed.

FAR RIGHT: Parodia chrysacanthion
RIGHT: Parodia aureispina

Pelargonium − Flowering

There are about 250 species of pelargonium, mainly from South Africa. However, those widely grown as flowering pot plants and for summer displays in our gardens, are hybrids that are the result of many years of intensive breeding.

Pelargonium grandiflorum (P. domesticum) hybrids

The result of crossing *P. grandiflorum*, *P. cordatum*, and other species. They are more popularly known as Regal or Martha Washington pelargoniums. The flowering season (early spring to mid summer) is shorter than in the zonal pelargoniums, but the blooms are larger, frillier, often more showy, and commonly bicoloured. The scalloped leaves with a serrated edge are about 7.5cm (3in) across and lack a distinctive zone. They make plants 30−60cm (1−2ft) tall in pots.

Pelargonium peltatum hybrids

Straggly, cascading stems, with shield-shaped, five-lobed leaves. Single or double, star-shaped flowers,

ABOVE LEFT: *A zonal pelargonium*
BELOW: *Regal pelargonium*

usually in shades of pink or red, sometimes white. Usually grown in a hanging basket or on a pedestal.

Pelargonium zonale hybrids

The traditional geraniums so widely grown as summer bedding. Rounded, slightly lobed leaves about 7.5−10cm (3−4in) across (smaller in miniatures), often attractively zoned and sometimes golden or variegated. Rounded heads of single or double flowers in shades of pink, orange, red, purple, and white. There are hundreds of varieties with variations in flower shape and size as well as colour and leaf patterning. Miniatures, growing only 15−23cm (6−9in) tall, are particularly useful for a windowsill.

HELPFUL HINTS

Temperature Winter minimum 7°C (45°F). Zonal pelargoniums will tolerate a few degrees lower, but are best maintained at the temperature recommended.
Humidity Tolerates dry air.
Position Good light with some sun.

Tolerates full sun.
Watering and feeding Water moderately from spring to autumn; pelargoniums they will tolerate dry soil more happily than most houseplants and are not demanding in this respect. Regal or Martha Washington pelargoniums need more water in summer than the other types. Feed regularly from spring to autumn.
Care Plants grown for the garden are often overwintered in a greenhouse, and kept in a semi-dormant state. Those grown as pot plants indoors can be kept in leaf and looking attractive if given sufficient − warmth at least 13°C (55°F) − and good light. Repot in spring if necessary. Deadhead regularly. Shorten long shoots in spring (autumn for Regal or Martha Washington types). Pinch out the growing tip of young plants to encourage bushy growth.
Propagation Cuttings; seed (some varieties).

ABOVE: Pelargonium peltatum *hybrid*
OPPOSITE: *Scented-leaved pelargoniums.*
Left to right: P. odoratissumum, P. graveolens, P. crispum *'Variegatum'*

Pelargonium – Foliage

Some of the zonal pelargoniums have attractive foliage as well as flowers, and are generally better looking than those grown specifically for their scented leaves. Pelargoniums with scented leaves sometimes have small flowers but these tend to be unexciting, and the foliage itself is often uninspiring although some varieties are variegated. They are grown for the strong aromas released when you brush against the leaves (and sometimes even when you don't).

Descriptions used to classify the scents sometimes appear to contradict one another, at other times to be fanciful, but this is largely because scent can be perceived differently from one person to another, and some of the plants give off a blend or mixture of smells. The best way to choose scented species and varieties is simply to follow your nose.

A selection of different species is listed here, but you will find many more scented species and hybrids at specialist nurseries.

Pelargonium capitatum
Deeply lobed leaves, smelling of roses. Mauve flowers. Will grow to about 90cm (3ft) if conditions suit.

Pelargonium crispum
Small, slightly lobed, green and cream leaves, with a lemon fragrance. Pink flowers. Grows to about 60cm (2ft).

Pelargonium graveolens
Deeply divided, lobed leaves, smelling of roses. Pink to rose-red flowers. Grows to about 90cm (3ft).

Pelargonium odoratissimum
Apple-scented foliage. White flowers. Grows to about 30cm (1ft).

Pelargonium tomentosum
Large, rounded, slightly lobed leaves, smelling of peppermint. Small white flowers. Grows to about 60cm (2ft).

Pellaea

Deciduous, semi-evergreen or ever-green ferns, generally found in dry areas of South America, South Africa and New Zealand. Being adapted to dry conditions, most species are better able to cope with conditions found in the home than most other types of fern.

Pellaea rotundifolia

Small, round, leathery leaflets on long arching fronds that grow from a creep-ing rootstock. The leaflets become more oval in shape with age. Low, spreading growth.

Pellaea viridis

More like a traditional fern than the previous species, with larger and more divided feathery fronds.

HELPFUL HINTS

Temperature Aim for 13–16°C (55–60°F) in winter.

Humidity Mist the leaves occasional-ly. Although better adapted to dry conditions than most ferns, growth will usually be improved if reasonable humidity is provided.

Position Good light, but avoid ex-posing to direct sun.

Watering and feeding Water mod-erately at all times. Never allow the roots to dry out entirely, but avoid very wet compost (potting soil). Feed with a weak fertilizer in summer.

Care If repotting use a shallow con-tainer or a hanging basket. In the wild often grow in rock crevices.

Propagation Division; spores.

RIGHT: Pellaea rotundifolia
BELOW: Pellaea viridis

Pellionia

A small genus of evergreen creeping perennials, a few of which may be used in large terrariums or bottle gardens, or as trailers for a hanging pot.

Pellionia daveauana

Creeping plant with oval leaves, olive green around the edge with a pale

central area. You may also find it more correctly called *P. repens*.

Pellionia pulchra

Creeping plant with almost oblong leaves about 4–8cm (1½-3in) long and 2.5cm (1in) wide. These have a mottled appearance with dark green veins over an olive-green background, and the reverse is brownish-purple.

Pellonia repens *see P. daveauana.*

Temperature Winter minimum 13°C (55°F).
Humidity Mist the leaves regularly. Needs very high humidity.
Position Semi-shade or good light but no direct sun.
Watering and feeding Water freely from spring to autumn, sparingly in winter. Never allow the roots to become dry. Feed regularly in summer.
Care Misting alone is unlikely to provide sufficient humidity, so use other methods too, such as standing the pot over a dish of water, supporting the pot on marbles or pebbles to avoid direct contact.
Propagation Cuttings; division.

ABOVE: Pellionia daveauana

ABOVE: Pentas lanceolata

Pentas

A genus of about 30 mainly evergreen perennials and shrubs, generally found in areas such as the Middle East and tropical Africa.

Pentas carnea *see P. lanceolata.*

Pentas lanceolata

Small, star-shaped flowers in heads about 7.5–10cm (3–4in) across. Pink or red are the usual colours, but some varieties have white or mauve flowers. May be seen in flower in any month of the year, but winter is the most usual time. Hairy oval leaves about 5–7.5cm (2–3in) long. Also sold under its other name of *P. carnea.*

Temperature Winter minimum 10°C (50°F).
Humidity Mist occasionally.
Position Good light with some sun, but not direct summer sun during the hottest part of the day.
Watering and feeding Water freely from spring to autumn, sparingly in winter. Never allow the roots to become dry. Feed regularly in summer.
Care Pinch out the growing tips of young plants to make them bushy. If you want the plant for winter flowering, pinch out early buds that form in autumn. Repot annually in spring.
Propagation Cuttings; seed.

Peperomia

Peperomias form a large genus of about 1,000 species, mainly from tropical and subtropical America. Some are epiphytes that grow on trees, others terrestrial plants from tropical rain forests. Some are annuals, but most are evergreen perennials. Some of the most popular ones used as houseplants are listed below, but you may sometimes find others that are equally pleasing in the home. Most of those that you are likely to find are undemanding to grow, and their variation in leaf shape, colouring and size makes them interesting to collect. Small poker-like, creamy-white flower spikes are sometimes produced, but on most species these are of marginal interest and they are grown mainly as foliage plants.

Peperomia argyreia
Shield-shaped leaves with dark green

and silver blades and red stalks. Forms a neat, bushy clump. May also be found under its synonym *P. sandersii*.

Peperomia caperata
Heart-shaped leaves about 2.5cm (1in) long, deeply corrugated and grooved between the veins. Bushy, clump-forming growth. Varieties have variations in leaf shapes and colouring.

Peperomia clusiifolia
Leathery leaves about 7.5cm (3in) long, edged purple-red. *P. c.* 'Variegata' has cream and red margins. Upright growth to about 20cm (8in).

Peperomia fraseri
Circular to heart-shaped leaves, usually arranged in whorls on upright stems. The flower spikes are white and fragrant.

Peperomia glabella
Trailing stems with broadly oval,

glossy, bright green leaves.

Peperomia griseoargentea
Heart-shaped to almost circular leaves on long pinkish stalks. Deep corrugations between the veins create a quilted look. The under surface is pale green. You are also likely to find this plant sold under its other name of *P. hederaefolia* (or *P. hederifolia*).

Peperomia hederaefolia (also P. hederifolia) *see P. griseoargentea.*

Peperomia magnoliaefolia (also P. magnoliifolia) *see P. obtusifolia.*

Peperomia nummulariifolia *see P. rotundifolia.*

Peperomia obtusifolia
Thick, fleshy leaves about 5–10cm (2–4in) long, on short stalks. The plain green form is not often grown as there are several variegated varieties

with yellow or cream markings. Upright but sprawling growth to about 25cm (10in). The nomenclature of these plants is confused – you will sometimes find them sold as *P. magnoliaefolia* (or *P. magnoliifolia*), and while some experts consider them synonymous others list them as distinct species, whatever the label.

OPPOSITE: *Peperomias:* P. *hybrid 'Columbiana' (far left)*, P. *hybrid 'Rauvema' (second from left), and three varieties of* P. caperata
BELOW: *Peperomias:* P. pereskiifolia *(top left)*, P. obtusifolia *'USA' (top right)*, P. clusiifolia *'Jeli' (bottom left)*, P. clusiifolia *variety (bottom right)*

Peperomia pereskiifolia
Whorls of dull green leaves tinged dull red. Spread to 30cm (12in).

Peperomia rotundifolia
A trailing species with round, bright green leaves, about 1cm (½in) across. Also known as *P. nummulariifolia*.

Peperomia verticillata
Distinctive upright growth to about 30cm (1ft) with the 2.5cm (1in) leaves in whorls of four to six along the stems. Foliage covered with fine hairs.

HELPFUL HINTS
Temperature Winter minimum 10°C (50°F).

Humidity Mist the leaves occasionally in warm weather, not in winter.
Position Semi-shade or good light, but not direct summer sun.
Watering and feeding Water moderately throughout the year, cautiously in winter. Use soft water if possible. Feed from spring to autumn.
Care Most peperomias have only a small root system and annual repotting is unnecessary. When necessary, move to a slightly larger pot in spring. A peat-based (peat moss) compost (potting mixture) is preferable to one based on loam.
Propagation Cuttings; leaf cuttings from species with rosettes of fleshy leaves.

Philodendron

A genus of about 350 evergreen shrubs and woody climbers from the rain forests of Central and South America. Although most of the species listed here are climbers and will reach ceiling height, many are fairly slow-growing and will put on less than 30cm (1ft) in a year, so they will give years of pleasure before they outgrow their space. Some of the non-climbing species can make large, spreading plants, and may be too large for a small home.

Philodendron angustisectum
Vigorous climber with large heart-shaped leaves, about 45–60cm (1½-2ft) long, incised almost to the main rib. Will readily grow to ceiling height. May also be found under its other name of *P. elegans*.

Philodendron bipennifolium *see P. panduriforme.*

Philodendron bipinnatifidum
Non-climbing species with a straight stem densely clothed with leathery, heart-shaped, deeply lobed leaves about 45–60cm (1½-2ft) long. Will make a large plant that can be 1.8m (6ft) or more across and about 1.2m (4ft) tall.

Philodendron domesticum
Climber with glossy, bright green leaves about 30–45cm (1–1½ft) long, arrow-shaped on young plants but with more prominent basal lobes when it matures. Will readily reach ceiling height. Also listed under its alternative name of *P. hastatum*.

Philodendron elegans *see P. angustisectum.*

Philodendron erubescens
Climber with young leaves surrounded by attractive rose-red sheaths that drop as the foliage expands. Arrow-shaped to heart-shaped, dark green leaves with a purple sheen and red edge. There are also named selections

with either greener or redder foliage than in the normal plants. Will easily reach ceiling height.

Philodendron hastatum *see P. domesticum.*

Philodendron hybrids
There are hybrids and selections usually sold just by their varietal name, such as 'Blue Mink', 'Burgundy', and 'Pink Prince'. These are generally climbers with large, attractive leaves, and can be treated in the same way as the other climbing species listed here.

Philodendron melanochrysum
Climber with heart-shaped leaves about 60cm (2ft) long, with a coppery surface and white veins. Fairly slow-growing but will easily reach ceiling height. The heart-shaped leaves become increasingly elongated as the plant matures.

Philodendron panduriforme
Climber with leaves about 23–30cm (9–12in) long, deeply lobed, with a distinct 'waist' on mature foliage. May also be named *P. bipennifolium*.

Philodendron pertusum *see Monstera deliciosa.*

Philodendron scandens
Climber or trailer with 7.5–13cm (3–5in) heart-shaped, glossy green leaves. Fairly rapid growth and will reach ceiling height if given a support, but is most often seen as a trailer.

Philodendron selloum
A non-climbing species, with leaves 60–90cm (2–3ft) long, deeply incised and with ruffled edges. Grows to about 1.5m (5ft).

Helpful hints
Temperature Winter minimum 13°C (55°F), but many, such as *P. melanochrysum*, prefer warmer temperatures and for these 18°C (64°F) or higher is preferable.
Humidity Mist the leaves regularly.
Position Good light, but not direct summer sun. *P. scandens* tolerates low light levels well.
Watering and feeding Water freely from spring to autumn, moderately in winter. Use soft water if possible. Feed from spring to autumn, but avoid high-nitrogen feeds if you want to limit the plant's growth.
Care Provide a suitable support for climbing species – moss poles are a popular method. Aerial roots that form low down on the plant can be trained to grow into the pot.
Propagation Cuttings; air layering.

ABOVE: Philodendron scandens
RIGHT TOP: Philodendron *hybrid 'Red Emerald'*
RIGHT MIDDLE: Philodendron *hybrid 'Blue Mink'*
RIGHT BOTTOM: Philodendron domesticum
FAR RIGHT: Philodendron *hybrid 'Purple Prince'*

Phlebodium aureum

See Polypodium aureum.

Phoenix

A genus of about 17 palms. Most become large trees where they grow outdoors, but some can make attractive pot plants while young.

Phoenix canariensis
Feathery fronds, stiff and erect at first, arching later, with narrow leaflets.

Phoenix dactylifera
The edible date. Similar to previous species, but not normally grown as a houseplant.

Phoenix roebelenii
Gracefully arching fronds, on a compact plant that seldom grows larger than 1.2m (4ft).

HELPFUL HINTS
Temperature Winter minimum 7°C (45°F); 16°C (60°F) for *P. roebelenii.*

BELOW: Phoenix canariensis

Humidity Tolerates dry air.
Position Good light. Benefits from direct sun.
Watering and feeding Water moderately from spring to autumn, sparingly in winter. Feed regularly from spring to autumn.
Care Repot only when the plant becomes pot-bound as the plant resents unnecessary root disturbance. Roots often penetrate through the bottom of the pot, and for this reason these plants are often planted in deeper containers than normal. Trim off any dead or yellowing leaves that are spoiling the plant's appearance.
Propagation Seed; division for *P. roebelenii.*

Pilea

A genus of about 600 bushy or trailing annuals and evergreen perennials from tropical regions, a small number of which are grown as foliage houseplants.

Pilea cadierei
Elliptical to oval leaves about 7.5–10cm (3–4in) long, with silver markings that look as though they have been painted on the green background.

Pilea hybrids
Some pileas are likely to be found with just their varietal name. The botanical status of these is sometimes confused or debatable, and more than one species may have been involved in their breeding. These vary in colouring and variegation, but the general cultural advice given below applies to them.

Pilea involucrata
Oval, slightly fleshy leaves, about 5–7.5cm (2–3in) long and deeply quilted. The species has dark green foliage with a coppery sheen and pale green margins, but varieties include 'Moon Valley' (bronze above, reddish-green below), and 'Norfolk' (bronze in good light, almost green in poor light,

with several lengthwise white bands). You may find the latter listed as a variety of *P. spruceana.* They make bushy plants about 15–23cm (6–9in) tall.

Pilea microphylla
Small, pale green leaves only 2–6mm (⅛–¼in) long, on much-branched stems, forming a mass of fern-like foliage. Forms a dense, compact plant about 15cm (6in) tall. May also be found under its old name *P. muscosa.*

Pilea muscosa *see P. microphylla.*

Pilea nummulariifolia
Creeping reddish stems with round leaves about 1cm (½in) across, with a quilted surface, purplish on the underside. Grows to about 5cm (2in) tall.

ABOVE: Pilea microphylla
LEFT: Pilea spruceana *'Bronze' (left) and*
Pilea repens *(right)*
LEFT BELOW: Pilea cadierei

Pilea spruceana

Oval, wrinkled leaves 5–7.5cm (2–3in) long. Most likely to be seen in one of its varieties, such as 'Bronze'. 'Norfolk' is often listed as a variety of this species, but other authorities consider it a variety of *P. involucrata*.

HELPFUL HINTS

Temperature Winter minimum 10°C (50°F).
Humidity Mist the leaves regularly.
Position Good light or partial shade, out of direct summer sun.
Watering and feeding Water freely while in active growth. Feed regularly from spring to autumn.
Care Pinch out the growing tips of young plants, and repeat the process a month or two later, to encourage bushy growth. Repot in spring.
Propagation Cuttings.

Pinguicula

A genus of more than 50 species of insectivorous plants that work on the fly-paper principle.

Pinguicula grandiflora

Broad, flat, ground-hugging, spatula-shaped leaves about 7.5–10cm (3–4in) long, slightly curled at the edges.

BELOW: Pinguicula moranensis

Long-spurred pink flowers on slender stems about 10cm (4in) long, carried well above the foliage.

Pinguicula moranensis

Rounded to oval leaves about 15cm (6in) long. Crimson, magenta or pink flowers with white throat.

HELPFUL HINTS

Temperature Winter minimum 7°C (45°F).
Humidity Needs moderate humidity. Occasional misting is useful, but standing the plant in a water-filled saucer will also help.
Position Good light, but avoid exposing to direct sun.
Watering and feeding Water freely at all times. These plants are used to damp or bog conditions and will react badly if the roots become dry. This is one of the few plants that benefits if the saucer in which the pot stands is kept topped up with water so that the soil in the pot is always moist.
Care Do not worry if some of the older leaves start to die, as these are recycled by the plant and new leaves are formed. Provided the young leaves look healthy, the whole plant is in good health.
Propagation Division; leaf cuttings (lay cuttings on chopped sphagnum moss); seed.

Platycerium

A small genus of epiphytic ferns whose natural habitat is high up in trees in tropical rain forests. Usually grown in cultivation in a hanging basket or wired to a piece of cork bark.

Platycerium alcicorne *see P. bifurcatum.*

Platycerium bifurcatum
The roots are hidden behind shield-shaped, sterile fronds that appear to clasp the plant's support. The broad, fertile fronds, which stand forwards, are divided and look like a stag's antlers. The plant may also be found under the name *P. alcicorne.*

HELPFUL HINTS
Temperature Winter minimum 10°C (50°F), although a few degrees lower should not harm plants.
Humidity Mist the leaves occasionally, more often in hot weather, but it is not as vulnerable as most ferns in dry air.
Position Good light, but avoid exposing to direct sun.
Watering and feeding Water freely from spring to autumn, sparingly in winter. Use soft water if possible. Feed with a weak fertilizer while growing actively. If you are growing

ABOVE: Platycerium bifurcatum

the fern on a piece of cork bark in the home, the easiest way to water it is to plunge the bark and fern in a bucket of water, and then allow it to drain before rehanging.
Care Although it can be grown in a pot, this fern looks much better displayed in a more natural way. In a greenhouse or conservatory, hanging baskets are satisfactory, but in the home a piece of cork bark is a better choice. Drill holes and insert wires for hanging the cork bark and to hold the plant securely in place. Pack plenty of sphagnum moss around the root-ball and wire in position on the piece of bark.
Propagation Offsets; spores.

Plectranthus

A genus of trailing or bushy evergreen perennials. Most of those grown as houseplants have variegated foliage.

Plectranthus coleoides
Low-growing creeper with green, scalloped leaves about 5cm (2in) long. It is the variegated varieties that are normally grown. The leaves of 'Marginatus' have white margins. Now more correctly named *P. forsteri.*

P. forsteri *see P. coleoides.*

Plectranthus fruticosus
Light green, oval to heart-shaped leaves, with a scalloped edge, up to 15cm (6in) long, on stems that grow to about 90cm (3ft). Spikes of lilac-blue flowers may grow in winter.

Plectranthus oertendahlii
A creeping plant with oval to round leaves about 2.5cm (1in) across, green with white veins above, purple-red on the reverse.

HELPFUL HINTS
Temperature Winter minimum 10°C (50°F).
Humidity Mist occasionally.
Position Good light or semi-shade, but not direct sunlight.
Watering and feeding Water freely from spring to autumn, sparingly in winter. Feed from spring to autumn.
Care Pinch stems back to keep trailing varieties compact and bushy.
Propagation Cuttings.

BELOW: Plectranthus coleoides 'Marginatus'

ABOVE: Polypodium aureum

Polypodium

A large and diverse group of deciduous, semi-evergreen and evergreen ferns. The species described here is the one you are most likely to find grown as a houseplant.

Polypodium aureum
Blue-green, deeply-cut leaves sometimes 60cm (2ft) or more long. The creeping rhizomes are densely covered with orange-brown 'fur'. Although normally beneath the soil, these are sometimes visible. You may also find this plant sold or listed under its other name of *Phlebodium aureum*.

HELPFUL HINTS
Temperature Winter minimum 16°C (60°F).
Humidity Mist the leaves occasionally. Polypodium are more tolerant of dry air than most ferns.
Position Good light, but avoid exposing to direct sun.
Watering and feeding Water moderately from spring to autumn, sparingly in winter. Use soft water if possible. Feed regularly from spring to autumn.
Care Repot annually in spring.
Propagation Division of the rhizome; spores.

Polyscias

A genus of more than 70 evergreen trees and shrubs, a few of which are grown as houseplants. Unfortunately they can be difficult to grow successfully in the home.

Polyscias balfouriana
Leaves usually have three leaflets, which are dark green and speckled grey or paler green. Each leaflet, on a 15cm (6in) stalk, is about 7.5cm (3in) across and almost circular. 'Pennockii' has white veins, 'Marginata' has a white edge. Shrubby growth habit. Now considered to be more accurately named *P. scuttellaria* 'Balfourii'.

Polyscias fruticosa
Compound leaves usually with three leaflets, each about 15cm (6in) long and spiny-toothed, creating a feathery appearance. Makes a large bushy, upright plant in time.

HELPFUL HINTS
Temperature Aim for 13–16°C (55–60°F) in winter.
Humidity Mist the leaves regularly, and provide as much additional humidity as possible.
Position Good light, but avoid exposing to direct sun.
Watering and feeding Water freely from spring to autumn, moderately in winter. Use soft water if possible. Feed regularly in summer.
Care Use an ericaceous (lime-free) compost (potting soil) when you have to repot the plant.
Propagation Cuttings.

BELOW: Polyscias balfouriana

Polystichum

A large group of evergreen, semi-evergreen and deciduous ferns, distributed over most parts of the world. Many species are used as hardy garden plants, and the two listed below cannot withstand severe frosts.

Polystichum falcatum
Tough, glossy fronds 30–60cm (1–2ft) long with large leathery leaflets. 'Rochfordianum' has more numerous holly-shaped leaflets. Although classed as a polystichum by some, you are likely to find it sold as *Cyrtomium falcatum*, which is considered by other botanists to be its correct name.

Polystichum tsus-simense
Broadly lance-shaped, semi-evergreen fronds with delicate-looking, spiny-edged leaflets. Grows to a height of about 30cm (1ft).

HELPFUL HINTS
Temperature Winter minimum 5°C (41°F), although short periods below this are unlikely to be detrimental.
Humidity Mist the leaves regularly, although these plants are not as demanding as many other ferns.

Position Semi-shade or good light, but not direct sun.
Watering and feeding Water freely from spring to autumn, sparingly in winter. Feed regularly in summer.
Care Remove faded or damaged

ABOVE: Polystichum falcatum (*syn.* Cyrtomium falcatum) '*Rochfordianum*'

fronds to keep the plants looking at their most attractive.
Propagation Division; spores.

Primula

A large genus with about 400 species of annuals, biennials and perennials, many of them hardy garden plants. Those listed below are popular commercial pot plants which you are most likely to come across.

Primula acaulis *see P. vulgaris.*

Primula malacoides
Dainty flowers about 1cm (½in) across, arranged in two to six tiers along the flower stalk, in shades of pink, purple, lilac, red, and white, with a yellow eye. Flowers are carried on stems about 30–45cm (1–1½ft) tall, above toothed oval leaves. Winter flowering.

Primula obconica
Large, rounded heads of 2.5–4cm (1–1½in) flowers mainly in shades of pink and blue, on stems about 23–30cm (9–12in) tall, appearing in winter and spring. The pale green hairy leaves may cause an allergic reaction in some people.

Primula vulgaris hybrids
The true species is the common primrose, with yellow flowers nestling in the rosette of leaves. These are unsuitable as houseplants. The modern hybrids, however, have large, colourful blooms in many shades, mainly yellows, reds, pinks, and blues, most with a bold contrasting eye, on stems

RIGHT: Primula obconica

carried higher above the leaves than in the species. These are widely sold as pot plants, and although they are not suitable for long-term use indoors they make a pretty short-term display in winter and spring.

HELPFUL HINTS

Temperature Winter minimum 13°C (55°F). To prolong the display, avoid high temperatures while plants are in flower.
Humidity Mist the leaves occasionally, especially if the air is dry.
Position Good light with some sun, but no direct summer sun during the hottest part of the day.
Watering and feeding Water freely from spring to autumn, but sparingly in winter. Feed quite regularly during the flowering season using a weak fertilizer.
Care The *P. vulgaris* hybrids should be bought in flower or raised in a greenhouse and taken indoors once the buds begin to open. After flowering they are best discarded or planted in the garden. The other primulas listed here are also often treated as short-term plants raised afresh each year and discarded after flowering. You can, however, successfully keep *P. obconica* from year to year. Keep it cool and out of strong sunlight, and water sparingly during the summer when it has its resting period. Resume normal watering in autumn.
Propagation Seed.

Pteris

A genus of about 280 deciduous, semi-evergreen and evergreen ferns from tropical and subtropical regions around the world.

Pteris cretica

Deeply divided green fronds with slender, slightly serrated leaflets on arching stems, growing to about 30cm (1ft). There are many varieties and these are more often grown than the species. Examples are 'Albolineata'

(pale stripe down the centre of each leaflet), and 'Alexandrae' (variegated but with the ends of the leaflets cut and fringed).

Pteris ensiformis

Similar to the previous species, but with darker leaves. There are variegated varieties, such as 'Evergemiensis' (broad white lengthwise bands on the leaflets) and 'Victoriae' (similar to the previous variety but with less pronounced markings).

HELPFUL HINTS

Temperature Winter minimum 13°C (55°F) for plain green forms, 16°C (60°F) for variegated varieties.
Humidity Mist the leaves regularly.
Position Good light, but not direct sun. Plain green forms will tolerate poorer light than the variegated varieties.
Watering and feeding Water freely from spring to autumn, sparingly in winter. Use soft water if possible. Feed regularly with a weak fertilizer from spring to autumn.
Care Be especially careful never to allow the roots to become dry.
Propagation Division; spores.

ABOVE: Pteris ensiformis *'Evergemiensis'*
BELOW: Pteris cretica *'Albolineata'*

Radermachera

A small genus of vigorous evergeeen trees and shrubs native to South-east Asia. The species below is the only one you are likely to find.

Radermachera sinica

Doubly pinnate foliage with individual leaflets about 2.5cm (1in) long, distinctly pointed at the ends. Makes a bushy plant about 60cm (2ft) tall in most home conditions. May sometimes be listed or sold as *Stereospermum suaveolens*.

HELPFUL HINTS
Temperature Winter minimum 13°C (55°F).
Humidity Undemanding.
Position Good light, but not direct summer sun during the hottest part of the day.
Watering and feeding Water freely from spring to autumn, moderately in winter.
Care Pinch out the growing tip of a young plant to encourage more compact, bushy growth.
Propagation Cuttings.

RIGHT: Radermachera sinica

Rebutia

Cacti originating from northern Argentina and parts of Bolivia, where they grow at high altitudes. There are about 40 species.

Rebutia minuscula

Spherical body, usually about 5cm (2in) across and somewhat flattened. Short white spines. Red to orange-red flowers about 2.5cm (1in) long, in spring and early summer.

Rebutia pygmaea

Oval to finger-shaped ribbed body,

RIGHT: Rebutia senilis *(left) and* Rebutia miniscula *(right)*
FAR RIGHT: Rebutia pygmaea

with tiny spines. It is often only about 2.5cm (1in) tall, but old specimens will reach 10cm (4in). Purple, pink, or red flowers, about 2.5cm (1in) long, in late spring and early summer.

Rebutia senilis

A flattened sphere, densely covered with white thorns. Bright-red, trumpet-shaped flowers, over 2.5cm (1in) long, in spring and summer. There are varieties with yellow, lilac, and orange flowers. Grows to about 7.5cm (3in).

HELPFUL HINTS

Temperature Winter minimum 5°C (41°F).

Humidity Tolerates dry air, but appreciates a humid atmosphere in spring and summer.

Position Good light. Benefits from direct sun.

Watering and feeding Water moderately from spring to autumn, keep practically dry in winter. Feed in summer with a weak fertilizer or a special cactus food.

Care Repot in spring when it becomes necessary, using a cactus mixture.

Propagation Cuttings (from offshoots); seed.

Rhaphidophora aurea

See Epipremnum aureum.

Rhipsalidopsis

A small genus of epiphytic cacti from the tropical forests of southern Brazil.

Rhipsalidopsis gaertneri

Flattened, segmented stems bearing clusters of bell-shaped scarlet flowers with multiple petals in mid and late spring. May sometimes be listed as *Schlumbergera gaertneri*, and now considered by botanists to be more correctly named *Hatiora gaertneri*.

ABOVE: Rhipsalidopsis gaertneri (*syn.* Schlumbergera gaertneri)

HELPFUL HINTS

Temperature Winter minimum 10°C (50°F).

Humidity Mist leaves occasionally.

Position Good light, but not direct summer sun.

Watering and feeding Water freely while in active growth. In winter give sufficient water only to prevent the stems from shrivelling. Feed with a weak fertilizer in spring and summer.

Care A cool resting period is essential for good flowering – so avoid keeping the plant in a hot room in winter. Do not move the plant once the buds have formed. Stand in a shady spot outdoors for the summer months.

Propagation Cuttings; seed.

Rhododendron

A very large genus of evergreen and deciduous shrubs, ranging from small alpine species to large plants of tree-like stature. Many of them are hardy and popular garden plants, especially the hybrids. Only a couple of species have been developed as houseplants, however, and these are popularly known as azaleas.

Rhododendron × obtusum

Semi-evergreen, with glossy leaves 2.5–4cm (1–1½in) long. Single or double, funnel-shaped flowers in clusters of two to five blooms, in late winter and spring. Varieties are available in a range of colours. They usually grow 30–45cm (1–1½ft) tall when kept as a pot plant.

Rhododendron simsii

Evergreen leathery leaves, about 4–5cm (1½-2in) long. Profusion of 4–5cm (1½-2in) single or double flowers in a range of colours, mainly pinks and reds, as well as white, in winter and spring. They grow to about 30–45cm (1–1½ft) tall as a pot plant.

HELPFUL HINTS

Temperature Aim for 10–16°C (50–60°F) in winter.

Humidity Mist the leaves regularly.

Position Good light, but avoid exposing to direct sun.

Watering and feeding Water freely at all times, using soft water if possible. Feed regularly in summer.

Care Pay special attention to watering – plants are often sold in a very peaty (peat moss) mixture that is difficult to moisten once it dries out. Always use an ericaceous (lime-free) compost (potting soil) for repotting, which is best done about a month after flowering has finished. Place the plants in a shady and sheltered spot in the garden once all danger of frost is past. *R. × obtusum* varieties can be planted permanently in the garden in sheltered areas where the winters are not very severe. *R. simsii* varieties must be brought indoors again in early autumn. If you stand the plants in the garden, plunge the pots into the ground to conserve moisture – don't forget to keep them watered and fed.

Propagation Cuttings.

BELOW: Rhododendron × obtusum
BOTTOM: Rhododendron simsii

Rosa

Roses are universally popular plants, and although there are only about 200 different species, there are thousands of hybrids and varieties. However, even dwarf and miniature varieties make only short-term houseplants.

Rosa, miniature hybrids
A scaled-down rose 15–30cm (6–12in) tall, with single, semi-double, or double flowers about 1–4cm (½-1½in) across. They are available as bushes or trained as miniature standards. Most are derived from *R. chinensis* 'Minima', but the breeding of those available today is complex and they will usually be sold simply with a variety name, or perhaps just labelled 'miniature rose'. Some are true miniatures, growing less than 15cm (6in) high, but the treatment is the same however they are labelled when you buy them.

HELPFUL HINTS
Temperature Frost-hardy. Aim for 10–21°C (50–70°F) when the plants are growing actively.
Humidity Undemanding, but it is beneficial to mist occasionally.
Position Best possible light. Will tolerate full sun.
Watering and feeding Water freely from spring to autumn, while they are in leaf. Feed regularly in summer.
Care The plants are best kept outdoors for as long as possible. After flowering stand them on the balcony or patio and keep watered, or plunge the pot in the garden soil. Pots kept on a balcony or patio for the winter may need some protection to prevent the root-ball from freezing solid. Repot in autumn if necessary. Prune in spring as you would an ordinary rose – although with very small plants it may be sufficient simply to remove dead or crossing shoots. Bring indoors again in late spring, or as soon as flowering starts.
Propagation Cuttings.

RIGHT: *Rose, miniature hybrids*

Saintpaulia

A small genus of rosette-forming perennials, just one species of which is well known. The large colour range and variation in flower form are the result of introducing genes from other species such as *S. confusa*, although they are usually all listed as varieties of *S. ionantha*. The original species is not grown as a houseplant.

Most of the saintpaulias sold in shops and garden centres will lack a specific name, but if you go to a specialist supplier you will have a choice of hundreds of varieties, all accurately named.

The huge range of varieties available, in many colours and variations in flower form and growth habit, make saintpaulias an ideal plant for collectors. They can be induced to flower throughout the year if you can provide suitable light intensities.

Sizes
Large varieties grow to 40cm (16in) or more across. Standard saintpaulias are the ones most often bought and generally grow between 20–40cm (8–16in) across. Miniatures are only 7.5–15cm (3–6in) across. There are also varieties intermediate in size, and micro-miniatures less than 7.5cm (3in) across when mature. Trailers have more widely spaced foliage than normal varieties, with drooping stems that tend to arch over the pot.

Flower shapes
Single flowers are the most common type. Semi-double flowers have more than five petals, but the centre is still clearly visible. Double flowers have at least ten petals, and the yellow centre is not visible. Frilled flowers have petals with a wavy edge. Star flowers have five equally sized and spaced petals, instead of the more usual two small and three large petals.

Leaf shapes
These are just a few of the leaf shapes identified by specialists. Boy leaves are plain green, and do not have a spot at the leaf base. Girl leaves are the same shape as boy leaves, but have a small white spot or blotch at the base. Lance leaves are longer and more pointed at the end. Spoon leaves have a rolled-up edge. Variegated leaves are mottled or speckled with white or cream.

HELPFUL HINTS

Temperature Winter minimum 16°C (60°F).

Humidity Saintpaulias appreciate high humidity, but regular misting is not appropriate as water may lodge on the hairy leaves and cause rotting. Provide the humidity in other ways, such as standing the pot over a saucer of water on pebbles or marbles so that the compost (potting soil) is not in direct contact with the water.

Position Good light, but not direct summer sun during the hottest part of the day. Strong light without direct sun is ideal. Saintpaulias grow very well under suitable artificial light (at least 5,000 lux).

Watering and feeding Water freely from spring to autumn, moderately in winter, but never allow the roots to remain wet – try to let the soil surface dry out a little before watering again. Use soft water if possible. Try to

ABOVE, OPPOSITE TOP LEFT AND ABOVE LEFT: Saintpaulia hybrids

OPPOSITE BELOW: Saintpaulias, showing the diversity of flower shapes and colouring, including a double. A miniature is shown bottom right.

OPPOSITE ABOVE RIGHT: Saintpaulias: 'Maggie May' (left), 'Fancy Pants' (centre), 'Colorado' (right)

water without wetting the leaves – use the immersion method or direct the spout of the watering-can below the rosette of leaves. Feed during active growth. However, if the plant produces lots of leaves and few flowers despite adequate light, you may be overfeeding – switch to a low-nitrogen fertilizer.

Care Most windowsill plants flower in spring and summer, when the light is good, but by supplementing the light they will continue blooming for most of the year. If you have the ability to maintain high light levels, however, it is best to rest the plant for about a month: lower the temperature close to the minimum, reduce watering and shorten the day length. After a month, place in good light to start into active growth again. Remove any old leaves that are marring the plant.

Propagation Leaf cuttings; seed.

Sansevieria

A small genus of evergreen rhizomatous perennials with stiff, fleshy leaves. These are desert plants that can tolerate poor conditions.

Sansevieria trifasciata

Tough, sword-like leaves, slightly crescent-shaped in cross-section, that can be 1.5m (5ft) long in good conditions, but usually only grow to half this height in the home. Dull green leaves with paler cross-banding that creates a mottled appearance. A more popular form is the variety 'Laurentii' which has yellow leaf margins. 'Hahnii' is a low-growing variety with a short, funnel-shaped rosette of leaves; 'Golden Hahnii' is similar but with broad yellow stripes along the edge of each leaf. Spikes of white flowers are sometimes produced.

BELOW: Sansevieria trifasciata *'Laurentii'*

HELPFUL HINTS
Temperature Winter minimum 10°C (50°F).
Humidity Tolerates dry air.
Position Best in bright, indirect light, but will tolerate direct sun and also a degree of shade.
Watering and feeding Water moderately from spring to autumn, very sparingly in winter. Always allow the soil to dry out slightly before watering. Feed regularly in summer.
Care Repotting is seldom required, as plants respond well to cramped conditions. However, always repot if the roots show signs of splitting the pot.
Propagation Division; leaf cuttings (but yellow-edged varieties will revert to the green form).

Sarracenia

Carnivorous plants with just eight species in the genus. Demanding as a houseplant, but grown as a curiosity.

Sarracenia flava

Leaves like long trumpets, hooded at the top, grow to about 30–60cm (1–2ft) long indoors. Insects are lured into the trap, attracted by nectar in special glands, and by the yellow colouring developed by the leaf traps. They are digested by enzymes and bacteria. Unusual yellow or cream flowers are sometimes produced in spring.

Sarracenia purpurea

Rosette-forming plants with erect to semi-prostrate growth to about 30cm (12in). Inflated green traps with red or purple veins and markings. Purple flowers in spring.

HELPFUL HINTS
Temperature Winter minimum 5°C (41°F).
Humidity Mist the leaves regularly, and try to maintain a humid atmosphere around the plant.
Position Good light with or without direct sun, but not direct summer sun

ABOVE: Sarracenia purpurea

during the hottest part of the day.
Watering and feeding Water freely from spring to autumn (when the plant likes to be kept constantly wet), sparingly in winter. Feeding is not normally necessary.
Care The plant is likely to do better in a greenhouse or conservatory than in a centrally-heated living-room.
Propagation Seed.

Saxifraga

A large genus with hundreds of species, mostly alpines, but only one is commonly grown as a houseplant.

Saxifraga sarmentosa see *S. stolonifera*.

Saxifraga stolonifera

Rounded leaves about 4–5cm (1½–2in) across, broadly toothed, olive green with white veins above, reddish beneath. 'Tricolor' has green and red or pink leaves with silver or white markings, reddish beneath. Height is up to about 23cm (9in), but plantlets will cascade if grown in a hanging pot. May also be found under its older name of *S. sarmentosa*.

ABOVE: Saxifraga stolonifera

HELPFUL HINTS
Temperature Winter minimum 7°C (45°F).
Humidity Mist occasionally.
Position Good light, but avoid exposing to direct sun.
Watering and feeding Water freely from spring to autumn, sparingly in winter. Feed regularly in summer.
Care The species listed above is frost-hardy and will grow in the garden where winters are mild. 'Tricolor' is more delicate, however, and is best kept indoors. Trim off long runners if they look untidy.
Propagation Plantlets (peg down into pots).

Schefflera

A large genus of evergreen shrubs and trees, a few of which are grown as focal-point houseplants.

Schefflera actinophylla
Although a large tree where it grows outdoors, in the home it makes a bushy plant up to ceiling height. Large, spreading leaves with 5–16 leaflets (the older the plant, the more it is likely to have), each of them about 10–20cm (4–8in) long.

Schefflera arboricola
Erect, well-branched growth with 7–16 oval leaflets which radiate from the top of the leaf stalk like an umbrella. There are several widely available varieties with variegated foliage. You may also find this plant sold or listed as *Heptapleurum arboricola*.

HELPFUL HINTS
Temperature Winter minimum 13°C (55°F).
Humidity Mist the leaves regularly.
Position Good light, but avoid exposing to direct sun.

Watering and feeding Water freely from spring to autumn, sparingly in winter. Feed regularly in summer.
Care Can be trained as an upright, unbranching plant if you stake the plant and do not remove the growing tip, or can be made to bush out by removing the growing tip. Repot annually in spring.
Propagation Cuttings.

BELOW: Schefflera arboricola *'Aurea'*

Schizanthus

A small group of annuals from Chile. Most of the plants grown in pots are hybrids, evolved through many years of breeding by seed companies.

Schizanthus hybrids

Feathery, light green leaves, divided and fern-like in appearance. Exotic-looking, open-mouthed flowers, often described as orchid-like. Flowers multicoloured and very freely produced. Height depends on variety – dwarf varieties are most appropriate for the home, and you should be able to restrict them to little more than 30cm (1ft). Some greenhouse varieties grow to 1.2m (4ft).

HELPFUL HINTS

Temperature Aim for 10–18°C (50–64°F).
Humidity Mist occasionally.

BELOW: Schizanthus *hybrid*

Position Best possible light. Will tolerate some direct sun.
Watering and feeding Water freely at all times. Remember to feed regularly.
Care If raising your own plant, pinch out the growing tips while the seedlings are still young in order to produce bushy growth. Repeat again later if the plants seem to be lanky. Move younger plants into larger pots to avoid checking their growth. Avoid very high temperatures. Discard plants when flowering has finished.
Propagation Seed.

Schlumbergera

See Rhipsalidopsis and Zygocactus.

Scindapsus aureus

See Epipremnum.

Sedum

A large genus of over 300 species, from temperate zones throughout the world. Many of them are fleshy or succulent, including the majority of those used as pot plants.

Sedum bellum

A small plant to about 7.5–15cm (3–6in), with leaves folded like buds that eventually spread apart and become spatula shaped. Small star-like white flowers in spring.

Sedum morganianum

Cascading growth with closely-packed grey-green, succulent cylindrical leaves that overlap like tiles, creating a tail-like appearance. Pink flowers may appear in summer.

ABOVE: Sedum sieboldii
'Mediovariegatum'
LEFT ABOVE: Sedum pachyphyllum
LEFT BELOW: Sedum × rubrotinctum

Sedum pachyphyllum

Erect with pale blue-green cylindrical leaves about 2.5cm (1in) long, slightly upturned and flushed red at the tips. Yellow flowers may appear in spring.

Sedum × rubrotinctum

Similar to the previous species, but more of the leaf tends to be flushed red, especially in strong sunlight.

Sedum sieboldii

Thin, flattish leaves, in groups of three, blue-green with a white edge. In the variety 'Mediovariegatum' the leaves have a central creamy-white blotch. Pink flowers may appear in late summer or autumn. Botanists have now moved this to another genus and called it *Hylotelephium sieboldii*, but it is still sold as a sedum.

HELPFUL HINTS
Temperature Winter minimum 5°C (41°F).
Humidity Tolerates dry air.
Position Best possible light.

Watering and feeding Water sparingly from spring to autumn, and keep practically dry in winter (water only to prevent the leaves from shrivelling up). Feeding is not normally necessary.
Care Repot in spring, using a potting soil that drains freely. A cactus mixture suits well.
Propagation Leaf cuttings (for varieties with large, fleshy leaves such as *S. pachyphyllum* and *S. morganianum*); stem cuttings.

Selaginella

A genus of about 700 species of moss-like perennials, most of them coming from tropical rain forests.

Selaginella kraussiana

Creeping stems with filigreed green foliage, yellowish-green in 'Aurea'. Individual stems may be 30cm (1ft) long, and they root readily as they spread over the surface.

Selaginella lepidophylla

Looks like a ball of rolled-up, dead foliage in its dry state (the form in which it is often sold as a curiosity plant). Within hours of being given water it opens to a rosette shape, and the green colouring gradually returns.

Selaginella martensii

Upright-growing stems to about 30cm (1ft), which later become decumbent and produce aerial roots. Frond-like sprays of feathery green foliage. There are variegated varieties, such as 'Watsoniana', which has silvery-white tips.

HELPFUL HINTS
Temperature Winter minimum 13°C (55°F).
Humidity Mist the leaves regularly. Additional humidity from other sources must be provided.
Position Partial shade – avoid direct sun all year round. Plants do well in bottle gardens and terrariums, where the atmosphere is humid and protected.
Watering and feeding Keep moist at all times, but reduce watering in winter to suit the lower temperatures. Feed occasionally in summer using a foliar feed.
Care Provide as much humidity as possible and avoid cold draughts and very hot, sunny windows. Do not be surprised if plants are short-lived in living-room conditions.
Propagation Division (pot up rooted pieces).

BELOW: Selaginella lepidophylla
BELOW LEFT: Selaginella martensii

Senecio

A very large group of plants, with over 1,000 species, distributed throughout the world. It includes plants as diverse as annuals and perennials, succulents and non-succulent perennials, ever-green shrubs, sub-shrubs and clim-bers. Relatively few are used as house-plants.

Senecio cruentus hybrids
Dense head of colourful daisy-like flowers in winter and spring. Colours include shades of red, pink, purple, white, and blue. Large, irregularly lobed, hairy leaves, which can almost be hidden when a compact plant is in full flower. Height ranges from about 23–75cm (9–30in), and flower size from 2.5–7.5cm (1–3in) depending on the variety. Choose compact varieties for the home. You will usual-ly find this plant called cineraria. Although botanists have now reclassi-fied it as *Pericallis cruenta*, it is not sold under this name.

Senecio macroglossus
Trailer or climber with small succu-lent, roughly triangular leaves re-sembling common ivy (*Hedera helix*). 'Variegatus' has white margins.

Senecio mikanioides
Trailer or climber similar to the pre-vious species, but the leaves have five

ABOVE: Senecio rowleyanus
BELOW: Senecio macroglossus
'Variegatus'

to seven sharply pointed lobes. Now reclassified as *Delairea odorata*.

Senecio rowleyanus
Trailer with pendent, thread-like stems clustered with pea-like leaves that resemble beads.

HELPFUL HINTS
Temperature Winter minimum 7°C (45°F). Try to keep *S. cruentus* varieties below 13°C (55°F).
Humidity Succulent types are toler-ant of dry air, but mist *S. cruentus, S. macroglossus*, and *S. mikanioides* occa-sionally.
Position Best possible light, but not direct sun for *S. cruentus. S. rowleyanus* should receive some direct sun. The other species listed here need good light but not direct summer sun, and

will tolerate semi-shade, but in winter provide as much light as possible.
Watering and feeding Water the non-succulent types freely from spring to autumn, sparingly in win-ter. Water *S. rowleyanus* sparingly at all times, and keep practically dry in winter. Feed all types when they are growing actively.
Care *S. cruentus* will die after flower-ing, so discard once blooming is over.
Propagation Although you can raise senecios from seed in the greenhouse, they are difficult to grow on from seed in the home. Most people buy them in flower if they cannot keep them in a greenhouse until flowering starts.

Sinningia

A small genus of tuberous perennials and deciduous sub-shrubs. Those com-monly grown are widely known and sold as gloxinias, and have been bred from *S. speciosa*.

Sinningia speciosa
Large, oval to oblong leaves arising directly from the tuber, about 20–25cm (8–10in) long and hairy. The underside is sometimes reddish. Large, showy, bell-shaped flowers ab-out 5cm (2in) long, in pink, red, blue, purple, or white, some with contrast-ing rim, others attractively speckled.

HELPFUL HINTS
Temperature Minimum 16°C (60°F) during growing season.
Humidity Mist around plants regu-larly, but avoid wetting the leaves or blooms. Provide as much humidity as possible by other methods.
Position Good light, but avoid ex-posing to direct sun.
Watering and feeding Water freely once the tubers have rooted well. Decrease watering at the end of the growing season (*see* Care). Feed reg-ularly in summer.
Care When flowering has finished, gradually reduce the amount of water given and stop feeding. Remove the

ABOVE: Sinningia speciosa

sometimes mottled. Height in flower is usually about 30–38cm (12–15in).

HELPFUL HINTS

Temperature Winter minimum 13°C (55°F).

Humidity Mist regularly, but try not to over-wet the leaves. Use soft water if possible.

Position Good light, but avoid exposing to direct sun.

Watering and feeding Water freely from spring to autumn, while plants are growing. Keep almost dry in winter if the top growth has died down. Feed regularly in summer.

Care After flowering, gradually reduce the amount of water given and stop feeding. Leave the rhizome in its old pot for most of the winter, but repot . and start into active growth again in late winter.

Propagation Division of rhizomes; leaf cuttings.

leaves when they have turned yellow. If you have space, store the tubers in the pot in a frost-free, place ideally at about 10°C (50°F).

Repot afresh in the spring, making sure you plant them the right way up and at about the same depth as before.

Propagation Leaf cuttings; seed.

Smithiantha

Only a few species are known, and these come from humid mountain forests in Mexico and Guatemala. These have been used to provide some attractive hybrids, however, that are especially worth growing if you have a conservatory. They are not easy to grow in a living-room.

Smithiantha hybrids

Loose heads of pendent, tubular flowers about 5cm (2in) long, with a slightly flared mouth, in autumn. Hairy, round to heart-shaped leaves, usually about 10cm (4in) long and

RIGHT: Smithiantha × hybrida

Solanum

A genus of about 1,400 species, from all parts of the world, and including annuals, perennials, shrubs, sub-shrubs and climbers. The only ones used in the home are the two species described below. These are grown for their decorative fruits, which are poisonous.

Solanum capsicastrum

A sub-shrub usually grown as an annual, generally reaching 30–60cm (1–2ft) as a pot plant, but this depends on variety. Lance-shaped leaves about 5cm (2in) long, and small white star-shaped flowers in summer. These are followed by egg-shaped or round green fruits that turn orange-red or scarlet by winter.

Solanum pseudocapsicum

Very similar to the previous species, but the stems are smoother and the fruits usually larger.

HELPFUL HINTS

Temperature Aim for 10–16°C (50–60°F) in winter.
Humidity Mist the leaves regularly.
Position Best possible light. Tolerates some direct sun.
Watering and feeding Water freely

BELOW: Solanum capsicastrum

throughout the growing period. Feed regularly in summer.
Care Most people buy the plants already in fruit, but they are easy to raise from seed. As they are uninteresting until the fruits colour, and conditions indoors are not really suitable, it is best to raise them in a greenhouse to take indoors later. If you want to try to keep an old plant, cut the stems back to half their length after flowering and water sparingly until spring, when you can repot the plant. Stand the plant in a garden frame or outside in the garden for the summer, but spray the flowers with water to try to assist pollination. Bring indoors in autumn, before the evenings turn cold.
Propagation Seed; cuttings.

Soleirolia

There is only one species in this genus, a native of Corsica. It is frost-hardy, but easily damaged or killed by hard winter frosts so is only suitable for growing outdoors in mild areas.

Soleirolia soleirolii

Creeping, ground-hugging plant with very small round leaves that give a mossy appearance from a distance. The species itself is green, but there are silver and gold varieties that masquerade under several names. The silver form 'Variegata' is also sold as 'Argentea' and 'Silver Queen'. The golden form 'Aurea' is also sold as 'Golden Queen'. They all grow to form compact mounds not more than 5cm (2in) tall. You are also likely to find the plant under its older name of *Helxine soleirolii*.

HELPFUL HINTS

Temperature Frost-hardy, but aim for 7°C (45°F) when growing it as a pot plant.
Humidity Mist the leaves regularly.
Position Good light, but avoid exposing to direct sun.
Watering and feeding Water freely

TOP AND ABOVE: Soleirolia soleirolii

at all times. Feeding is normally unnecessary.
Care Repot in spring. A low, wide
container is better than a normal pot,
as the growth quickly spreads and
hangs over the edge.
Propagation Division.

Solenostemon

See Coleus.

Sparmannia

A small group of evergreen trees and
shrubs. The only species normally
grown as a pot plant is the one
pictured and described on this page,
Sparmannia africana.

Sparmannia africana
Large, pale green downy leaves up to
25cm (10in) across. Long-stalked clusters of white flowers with yellow and
purplish-red stamens in spring. Makes
a large plant that will reach ceiling
height.

HELPFUL HINTS
Temperature Winter minimum 7°C
(45°F).
Humidity Mist occasionally.
Position Good light, but not direct
summer sun during the hottest part of
the day.
Watering and feeding Water freely
from spring to autumn, sparingly in
winter. Feed regularly in spring and
summer.
Care Cut back the stems when flowering is over — this helps to keep the
plants compact and may encourage a
later flush of flowers. When you repot, you can cut it back severely to a
height of about 30cm (1ft) if necessary. Young plants may need repotting several times in a year. The plant
can be stood outdoors for the summer,
but choose a sheltered position out of
direct sun, and bring indoors again
before the evenings turn cold. Pinch
out the growing tip of a young plant if
you want to encourage a bushy shape.
Propagation Cuttings.

RIGHT: Sparmannia africana

ABOVE: Spathiphyllum wallisii

Spathiphyllum

Rhizomatous evergreen perennials, grown for their arum lily-like flowers. Other species and hybrids are available, but the one below is compact and one of the most popular.

Spathiphyllum wallisii

Tuft-forming clusters of thin, lance-shaped leaves arising from soil level. Arum lily-type flowers with a sail-like white spathe and fragrant florets on a white spadix, in spring and sometimes autumn. Height 30–45cm (1–1½ft).

HELPFUL HINTS

Temperature Winter minimum 16°C (60°F).

Humidity Mist the leaves regularly. Provide additional humidity by other means too.

Position Best possible light in winter, semi-shade in summer, out of direct summer sun.

Watering and feeding Water freely from spring to autumn, sparingly in winter. Feed regularly in summer.

Care Pay special attention to providing high humidity, and avoid cold draughts. Repot annually, in spring.

Propagation Division.

Stapelia

A genus of about 100 clump-forming succulents, most of them from South and South West Africa.

Stapelia variegata

Angular, fleshy green stems arising from the base of the plant and forming a small clump, usually about 10–15cm (4–6in) long. Star-shaped flowers about 5–7.5cm (2–3in) across, variable in colour but usually blotched or mottled yellow, purple, and brown, appearing in summer or autumn. Now reclassified as *Orbea variegata*, but likely to be sold as a stapelia.

HELPFUL HINTS

Temperature Winter minimum 10°C (50°F).

Humidity Tolerates dry air.

Position Best possible light.

Watering and feeding Water freely from spring to autumn, sparingly in winter. Feeding not necessary if plant is repotted periodically.

Care Repot in spring, annually if growth is good.

Propagation Cuttings; seed.

BELOW: Stapelia variegata

ABOVE: Stephanotis floribunda

Stephanotis

A small genus of climbers. The species described below is the one most commonly grown. This is a popular plant for bridal bouquets in some countries.

Stephanotis floribunda

Glossy, oval leaves 7.5–10cm (3–4in) long. Clusters of very fragrant star-shaped tubular white flowers in spring and summer. Will reach 3m (10ft) in good conditions. Often trained around wire hoops as a small plant, but is a vigorous climber requiring a proper support in a conservatory.

HELPFUL HINTS

Temperature Aim for 13–16°C (55–60°F) in winter. Avoid high winter temperatures.

Humidity Mist occasionally.

Position Best possible light, but not direct summer sun during the hottest part of the day.

Watering and feeding Water freely from spring to autumn, sparingly in winter. Feed regularly in summer, only in moderation if the plant is already large and seems too vigorous.
Care Train plant to a support. Shorten over-long shoots in spring, and cut out overcrowded stems at the same time. Repot every second spring.
Propagation Cuttings.

Stereospermum suaveolens

See Radermachera sinica.

Strelitzia

A small genus of large and exotic-looking plants from South Africa. Only the species described here is grown as a houseplant.

Strelitzia reginae
Clump-forming with large paddle-shaped leaves about 90cm (3ft) tall, including the stalk. Spectacular and long-lasting orange and blue flowers sitting in a boat-like bract. Spring is the main flowering period, but they may bloom at other times.

HELPFUL HINTS
Temperature Aim for a winter temperature of 13–16°C (55–60°F).
Humidity Mist occasionally.
Position Best possible light, but not direct summer sun during the hottest part of the day.
Watering and feeding Water freely from spring to autumn, sparingly in winter. Feed regularly from spring to autumn.
Care Repot as infrequently as possible as the roots are easily damaged. Be patient if you buy a small plant or raise your own from seed, as they can take four or five years to flower.
Propagation Division; seed.

BELOW: Strelitzia reginae

Streptocarpus

A genus of woodland plants from South Africa and Madagascar, but the ones grown in the home are almost always hybrids.

Streptocarpus hybrids

Long, stemless, strap-shaped leaves, 20–30cm (8–12in) long, growing more or less horizontally and often arching over the edge of the pot. Trumpet-shaped flowers about 5cm (2in) across in shades of pink, red, and blue, on stems about 23cm (9in) tall. Late spring to late summer is the normal flowering time. The leaf sap sometimes causes an irritating rash.

Streptocarpus saxorum

Woody-based perennial with whorls of small, oval, hairy leaves. Lilac flowers, like a smaller version of the hybrids, in summer and autumn.

HELPFUL HINTS
Temperature Winter minimum 13°C (55°F).
Humidity Mist the leaves occasional-ly, lightly so as not to soak them.
Position Good light, but not direct summer sun.
Watering and feeding Water freely from spring to autumn, sparingly in winter. Feed regularly in summer.
Care Benefits from a dormant winter season, with the compost (potting soil) only slightly moist and the temperature close to the minimum suggested. Repot in mid spring.
Propagation Leaf cuttings; seed.

Stromanthe

A small genus, from the maranta fami-ly, native to tropical regions of South America. They are easily confused with some species of ctenanthe and calathea.

Stromanthe amabilis

Pale green oval leaves, attractively cross-banded either side of the midrib with grey streaks. The reverse of the leaf is grey-green. This has now been reclassified as *Ctenanthe amabilis*.

Stromanthe sanguinea

Stiff, erect growth, with glossy, lance-shaped leaves about 38cm (15in) long, olive green above with a pale central vein. The reverse is purplish-red. Many-stemmed flower heads may be produced in spring. The true flowers are small and white, but the conspi-cuous bracts are vivid scarlet.

HELPFUL HINTS
Temperature Winter minimum 18°C (64°F).
Humidity Mist the leaves regularly,

ABOVE: Stromanthe amabilis
OPPOSITE ABOVE: Streptocarpus
saxorum
OPPOSITE BELOW: Streptocarpus *hybrid*

and supplement with other methods of raising the humidity level.
Position Good light, but not direct summer sun during the hottest part of the day.
Watering and feeding Water freely from spring to autumn, sparingly in winter. Use soft water if possible. Feed regularly in summer.
Care These are difficult plants to care for indoors. If you have a heated greenhouse or conservatory, keep them there for most of the year, only bringing them into the home for short periods. When repotting, use a soil mixture that drains freely.
Propagation Division.

Syagrus weddeliana

See Cocos weddeliana.

Syngonium

A genus of about 30 species, from tropical rain forests in Central and South America. These woody climbers have leaves that change shape according to the plant's stage of growth, and adult leaf forms are often much more lobed than the juvenile forms usually seen on small pot plants.

Syngonium podophyllum

Foot-shaped compound leaves, arrow-shaped on young plants. There are several variegated varieties, the main differences being in the position and extent of the cream or white markings. Some leaves are almost entirely white or yellow. Grows to about 1.8m (6ft) with a suitable support.

HELPFUL HINTS
Temperature Winter minimum 16°C (60°F).

Humidity Mist the leaves regularly.
Position Good light, but not direct sun. Tolerant of low light levels.
Watering and feeding Water freely from spring to autumn, sparingly in winter. Feed regularly in spring and summer.
Care If you prefer the juvenile foliage, cut off the climbing stems that develop – the plant will remain bushy rather than climb, and the leaves will be more arrow-shaped. Repot every second spring.
Propagation Cuttings; air layering.

BELOW: Syngonium *hybrid 'White Butterfly'*

Tillandsia

About 400 species of mainly epiphytic plants. Many of those that derive nutrients from air alone are now popular as novelty plants, and are often used as decorations even by non-gardeners. These are usually displayed for sale glued or wired to accessories such as shells, mirrors or pieces of wood. A few of the species planted in pots are grown for their interesting or unusual flowers.

Air plant tillandsias

These interesting plants have special scaly leaves, capable of trapping moisture from the air, and they can even absorb nutrients from dust and any nutrient-rich moisture that may be about. *T. usneoides* grows best in a humid greenhouse, but the other species listed here are compact and tough enough to grow in the home.

The scales that give the air plants their unique quality reflect light in such a way that the plants all tend to look grey in colour. For that reason they are sometimes referred to as the grey tillandsias. The species listed here provide a cross-section of some of the most popular, but specialist suppliers will offer many more.

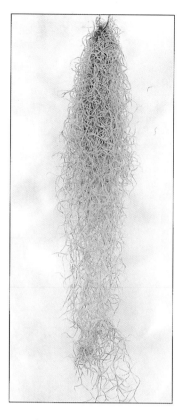

Tillandsia argentea
Rosettes of very narrow, thread-like leaves, with a bulb-like base. Loose sprays of small red flowers may appear in summer.

Tillandsia caput-medusae
Thick, twisted, reflexed leaves, broadening at the base to form a bulb-like structure. Quite showy red flowers in blue bracts in summer.

Tillandsia ionantha
Compact rosettes of silvery arching leaves. The inner leaves turn red when the small spikes of violet-blue flowers emerge in summer.

Tillandsia juncea
Tufts of rush-like foliage reflexing outwards, forming a thick, bushy rosette.

Tillandsia magnusiana
Thread-like leaves covered in grey scales, bulbous at base.

Tillandsia oaxacana
Dense rosette of rolled grey-green foliage. Flowers not a feature.

Tillandsia usneoides
Cylindrical leaves about 5cm (2in) long on slender drooping stems. Forms a long cascading chain of grey leaves suspended from the plant's support. There are inconspicuous yellowish-green flowers in summer, which tend to be lost among the foliage.

OPPOSITE FAR LEFT: Tillandsia usneoides
OPPOSITE ABOVE: Tillandsia magnusiana
OPPOSITE MIDDLE: *Tillandsias. From left to right:* T. oaxacana, T. caput-medusae, T. juncea, *and* T. ionantha
OPPOSITE BELOW: Tillandsia argentea

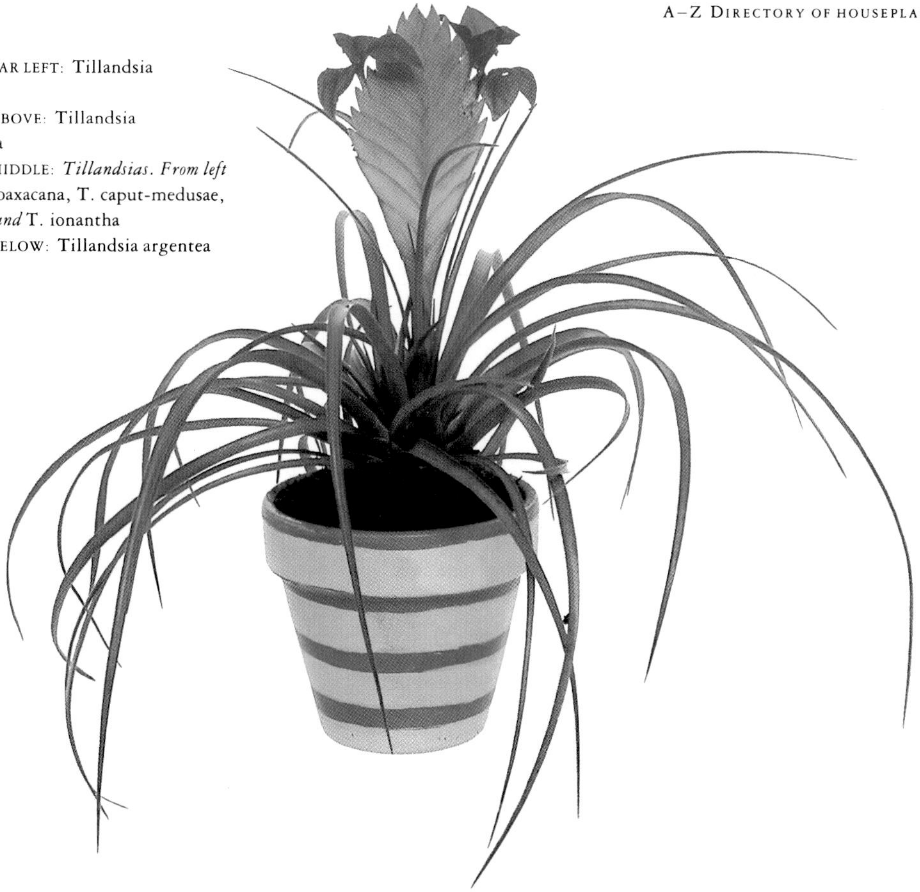

Flowering pot tillandsias

Tillandsias grown for their flowers are very different in appearance to air plant species. Although their root systems are not extensive, they are grown in pots like a conventional houseplant.

Tillandsia cyanea
Rosette of narrow, grass-like leaves, reddish-brown at the base and striped brown along the length. Blade-like flower spike in summer, from which purple-blue, pansy-shaped flowers appear along the edge of the spike from the pink or red bracts. The plant grows to about 25cm (10in).

Tillandsia lindenii
Similar to the previous species, but the blue flowers have a white eye.

HELPFUL HINTS
Temperature Winter minimum 13°C (55°F) for air plant tillandsias, 18°F (64°F) for the flowering species.
Humidity Mist regularly. This is especially important for the air plants, as these depend on atmospheric moisture. If possible, provide additional humidity by other methods as well.
Position Good light, but not direct sun in summer. The air plants can tolerate quite low light levels.
Watering and feeding Air plants receive their moisture by regular – preferably daily – misting. Water the other species freely from spring to autumn, sparingly in winter. Use soft water if possible. Air plants are fed via the leaves using a mister, but use a very weak solution of the fertilizer, and only apply when the plants are growing actively. Feed pot-grown species in the same way, or by adding the fertilizer to the soil.
Care Air plants are often wired into position on a bromeliad 'tree' or suitable support. If you want to fix them to a mirror or ornament, use adhesives sold for the purpose by many garden centres. Other species can be potted in spring. Although the flowered part will die, other shoots will appear.
Propagation Offsets.

ABOVE: Tillandsia cyanea

Tolmiea

ABOVE: Tolmiea menziesii

The single species below is the only one in the genus, a native of the west coast of North America. It is hardy enough to be grown in the garden.

Tolmiea menziesii
Bright green foliage arranged in a rosette and forming a mound of heart-shaped lobed leaves about 5cm (2in) across. The leaf stalks are long and when the plant is grown in a hanging pot this sometimes gives the plant a cascading appearance. Young plantlets form at the base of the leaf blade. 'Taff's Gold' is a variegated variety that you may also find under the names 'Goldsplash', 'Maculata', and 'Variegata'. It is sometimes semi-evergreen.

HELPFUL HINTS
Temperature Hardy, but usually requires a winter minimum of 5°C (41°F) when grown as a houseplant. Avoid high winter temperatures.
Humidity Mist occasionally.
Position Good light or semi-shade, but not direct sun.

Watering and feeding Water freely from spring to autumn, sparingly in winter. Feed regularly in summer.
Care If the plant becomes too large and its stems are congested, try cutting it back in spring to allow new leaves to grow from the base. Repot annually in spring. The plant can be stood outside for the summer, but choose a position out of direct sun.
Propagation Division, or pot up plantlets.

Tradescantia

A genus of about 70 species, including hardy border plants as well as tender trailers. It now includes *Zebrina pendula*, another popular trailing houseplant.

Tradescantia albiflora *see T. fluminensis.*

Tradescantia blossfeldiana
Narrowly oval, slightly fleshy leaves 5–10cm (2–4in) long in two distinct rows on hairy, trailing stems. In the species the leaves are glossy green above and sometimes tinged purple beneath. It is the variegated varieties that are usually grown, however, and 'Variegata' has longitudinal cream stripes. The flowers are pink with a white base. This species is now more correctly *T. cerinthoides*.

Tradescantia cerinthoides *see T. blossfeldiana.*

Tradescantia fluminensis
Trailing, rooting, hairless stems, with short-stalked green leaves about 5–7.5cm (2–3in) long, sometimes tinged purple beneath. It is the variegated varieties that are grown, however, and these include 'Albovittata' (creamy-white lengthwise stripes), 'Quicksilver' (clear white markings), and 'Tricolor' (white and pale purple stripes). The white flowers are unspectacular. This species was once considered distinct from *T. albiflora* (colourless sap in *albiflora*, violet in *fluminensis*), but they are now classed by botanists as one species. You may find them under either name.

Tradescantia zebrina

Pointed oval leaves about 5cm (2in) long on creeping or trailing stems. The upper surface is pale green with a silvery sheen and lengthwise purple stripe, and the underside is purple. Small white or rose-red flowers. This plant is still widely known and sold as *Zebrina pendula*. The variety 'Purpusii' is a little larger and more robust, with purple-tinged, bluish-green leaves and pink flowers. This is likely to be found also as *Zebrina purpusii* or *Tradescantia purpusii*.

HELPFUL HINTS

Temperature Keep temperature in

LEFT: Tradescantia blossfeldiana *'Variegata'*
BELOW: Tradescantia fluminensis *'Albovittata'*
BOTTOM: Tradescantia zebrina

winter to a minimum of 7°C (45°F).
Humidity Mist occasionally.
Position Good light, including some direct sun. Variegation will be inferior in poor light.
Watering and feeding Water freely from spring to autumn, sparingly in winter. Feed regularly from spring to autumn.
Care The plants soon look untidy with tangled growth, and if conditions are not good the leaves may turn brown or shrivel. Trim them back by pinching out unattractive shoots – this will encourage bushy new growth from near the base.
Propagation Cuttings.

Tulipa

Although there are only about 100 species of tulip, breeding has produced a huge range of hybrids and varieties that are planted in their millions every year. None of them can be considered true houseplants, but some are forced for early flowering in winter and may be used as a short-term houseplant.

Tulipa hybrids

The tulip needs no description, but there are many kinds. Consult a good bulb catalogue for those varieties suitable for growing in pots for early flowering – these will usually be compact types such as early singles and early doubles, and specialists will also offer bulbs that have been specially treated or 'prepared' so that they come into flower early. Florists and garden centres also offer pots of tulips that are just coming into flower, and these are a useful option.

HELPFUL HINTS

Temperature Hardy, and once in flower the cooler the room, the longer the flowers should last. See below for advice on earlier treatment.
Humidity Undemanding.
Position If brought indoors just as the flowers open, they can be placed anywhere you choose.

ABOVE: *Tulip, early double*

Watering and feeding Water moderately while in the home.
Care In early or mid autumn, plant the bulbs with their necks just below the compost (deep planting is impractical in a pot). Place in a sheltered position outdoors, and cover with fine gravel, pulverized bark, or some other suitable mulch, to a depth of at least 5cm (2in). Keep the soil in the pots just moist but be careful not to overwater. When the shoots are about 4–5cm (1½-2in) tall, or as soon as you can detect signs of a bud, bring into the light. Keep the pots in a light place at about 15°C (59°F) – ideally in a greenhouse or conservatory – until the buds show colour. Then bring them into the home. Discard or plant in the garden once flowering is over.
Propagation Bulb offsets, but this is not a practical option in the home. Buy fresh bulbs each year.

Veltheilmia

There are only a handful of species in this genus of bulbous plants, which originate from South Africa.

Veltheilmia capensis

Strap-shaped, wavy-edged leaves about 30cm (1ft) long. The flower spike, consisting of about 60 small, bell-like, pink or red blooms, arises from the centre of the plant in winter.

ABOVE: Veltheilmia capensis

HELPFUL HINTS

Temperature Winter minimum 10°C (50°F), but at higher than 13°C (55°F) the flowers tend to drop.
Humidity Undemanding.
Position Good light, including sun in winter.
Watering and feeding Water cautiously until growth appears, moderately throughout the growing period, then gradually reduce the amount of water given in late spring or early summer. The leaves will then die down as the bulb enters its dormant period.

Once growth is well established, feed regularly until flowering is over.
Care Plant the bulbs in autumn, and keep at about 21°C (70°F) until growth starts. After the bulbs have flowered and entered their resting period, keep the pots practically dry until early autumn. During the dormant stage you can stand the pots in a sheltered position outdoors.
Propagation Bulb offsets; seed (slow).

Vriesea

Bromeliads with about 250 species in the genus, occurring naturally in Central and South America.

Vriesea hieroglyphica

A species grown for foliage effect. Large rosette of wide, strap-shaped leaves with very dark green, sometimes almost black, markings. Seldom flowers in cultivation.

Vriesea hybrids

Hybrids are sometimes available ('Elan' is illustrated). Others include 'Perfecta' (a cross between V. *carinata* and V. 'Poelmannii') and 'Poelmannii' (a cross between V. *gloriosa* and V. *vangertii*).

OPPOSITE ABOVE: Vriesea splendens
LEFT: Vriesea *hybrid 'Elan'*

Washingtonia

A very small genus of just two species of tall palms. Both are occasionally used as a houseplants, but the species described below is the one you are most likely to find.

Washingtonia filifera
Fan-shaped, long-stalked, grey-green leaves with fibrous threads at the ends. Will make a large specimen if conditions suit, but is often short-lived in the home.

BELOW: Washingtonia filifera

Vriesea splendens
Rosette of arching, strap-shaped leaves, 30–45cm (1–1½ft) long on a mature plant, with brown cross-bands. The bright red flower head, 60cm (2ft) long, rises above the rosette of leaves. The true flowers are yellow but the plant is grown for the colourful red bracts, which appear mainly in summer and autumn.

HELPFUL HINTS
Temperature Winter minimum 15°C (59°F).
Humidity Mist the leaves regularly.
Position Light shade or good light out of direct sun.
Watering and feeding Water freely from spring to autumn, sparingly in winter. Keep the 'vase' formed by the leaves topped up with water from mid spring to mid autumn. Use soft water if possible. Feed with a weak fertilizer in summer.
Care The species grown for their colourful flower spikes are often discarded after flowering, but offsets will form around the old plant and these can be grown on to flower in due course. They are difficult to grow successfully in the home throughout their lives, however. If repotting, use an ericaceous (lime-free) mixture. You can also grow them attached to a bromeliad 'tree' made from an old branch, if you have space.
Propagation Offsets.

HELPFUL HINTS
Temperature Winter minimum 10°C (50°F).
Humidity Undemanding.
Position Best possible light, with some direct sun, but avoid sunlight through glass during the hottest part of the day in summer.
Watering and feeding Water freely from spring to autumn, sparingly in winter. Feed regularly in summer.
Care The plant will appreciate being stood outside, perhaps on the patio, for the warmest months. In winter, the plant is better in a cool conservatory than in a living-room.
Propagation Seed (difficult).

Yucca

A genus of about 40 species of evergreen trees and shrubs, some of which are hardy. The two species listed below are the ones most commonly seen as houseplants.

Yucca aloifolia

The leaves, up to 50cm (20in) long, grow in a dense rosette, and have very sharp points. A pronounced trunk gives it a tree-like shape.

Yucca elephantipes

Similar to the previous species, but the leaf tips are not sharp. This is the species commonly sold, and in Europe large quantities of the sawn stems are imported from countries such as Honduras. These 'trunks' are then started into growth like giant cuttings, to produce attractive plants with a thick trunk. Commercial growers sometimes refer to this species as *Y. elegantissima* but you are unlikely to see this name used.

HELPFUL HINTS

Temperature Winter minimum 7°C (45°F).
Humidity Tolerates dry air.
Position Good light with some sun.
Watering and feeding Water freely

BELOW: Yucca elephantipes

from spring to autumn, sparingly in winter. Feed regularly in summer.
Care Repot small plants if necessary, large ones can remain in the same container for many years, but in this case it is worth removing and replacing the top 2in (5cm) of the compost (potting mixture). The plant will be happy standing on the patio for the summer, but keep in shade for the first few weeks to acclimatize.
Propagation Sideshoots can be used as cuttings. The large-trunked plants seen in shops are raised from imported stems.

Zebrina

See Tradescantia.

Zephyranthes

A genus of bulbous plants from Central and South America. Growing plants are not often sold, but you can obtain the bulbs easily from specialist bulb companies.

Zephyranthes candida

Fine, grass-like leaves, and crocus-like white flowers, sometimes with a hint of purple, in autumn. Grows to about 15cm (6in).

BELOW: Zephyranthes grandiflora

ABOVE: Zephyranthes candida

Zephyranthes grandiflora

Similar to the previous species but with larger, rosy-pink flowers with a yellow throat on 30cm (1ft) stems, in early summer.

HELPFUL HINTS
Temperature Winter minimum 5°C (41°F).
Humidity Undemanding.
Position Best possible light, with some direct sun.
Watering and feeding Water freely when the bulbs are growing actively, sparingly when they are resting. Never let the soil become completely dry even during the resting period.
Care If necessary, repot when the bulbs are dormant, but do not repot unnecessarily. The display is usually better when the pot is densely planted with bulbs.
Propagation Division; seed.

Zygocactus

Forest cacti with flattened stems. The plants widely grown for the home are hybrids of Z. truncatus, but you may

also find them allocated to the genus schlumbergera. Some may be hybrids between more than one genus.

Zygocactus truncatus hybrids

Flattened, winged segments forming arching branches. Exotic-looking flowers with two tiers of reflexed petals and forward-thrusting stems and stigma. The flowers, up to 7.5cm (3in) long, are borne on the tips of the shoots. Bright violet flowers are most common, but they vary from orange to lilac, as well as white. Late autumn and winter are the main flowering times. Also labelled under what some consider to be their more correct name of *Schlumbergera truncata*.

HELPFUL HINTS
Temperature Winter minimum 13°C (55°F).
Humidity Mist the leaves regularly.
Position Good light, but not direct summer sun.
Watering and feeding Water freely from late autumn, sparingly from late winter onwards. Increase the amount of water given again when buds start to form in the autumn. Use soft water if possible. Feed with a weak fertilizer during the period of active growth.
Care Stand the plant outdoors in a shady spot for the summer, but bring in before the evenings turn too cold. Avoid turning or moving the plant once the buds are well developed as they may drop. Repot young plants each spring, mature ones only every second or third year.
Propagation Cuttings.

BELOW: Zygocactus truncatus (*syn.* Schlumbergera truncata)

Index of common plant names

African hemp – *Sparmannia africana*
African violet – Saintpaulia
Air plant – Tillandsia
Aluminium plant – *Pilea cadierei*
Amaryllis – Hippeastrum
Angel's trumpet – *Datura suaveolens* (syn. *Brugmansia suaveolens*)
Arabian violet – *Exacum affine*
Arrowhead vine – *Syngonium podophyllum*
Artillery plant – *Pilea microphylla*
Asparagus fern – *Asparagus densiflorus*, A. *plumosus* (syn. A. *setaceus*)
Autumn crocus – Colchicum
Azalea, Indian – *Rhododendron simsii*
Azalea, Japanese – *Rhododendron obtusum*
Baby rubber plant – *Peperomia clusiifolia*
Baby's tears – *Helxine soleirolii* (syn. *Soleirolia soleirolii*)
Ball cactus – *Parodia chrysacanthion*
Banyan tree – *Ficus benghalensis*
Barberton daisy – Gerbera
Barrel cactus – *Echinocactus grusonii*
Basket begonia – *Begonia tuberhybrida* 'Pendula'
Bead plant – *Nertera granadensis* (syn. N. *depressa*)
Beefsteak plant – *Iresine herbstii*
Begonia, fibrous-rooted – *Begonia semperflorens*
Begonia vine – *Cissus discolor*
Bellflower – Campanula
Bengal fig – *Ficus benghalensis*
Bird's nest bromeliad – *Nidularium innocentii*
Bird's nest fern – *Asplenium nidus*
Bird of paradise – *Strelitzia reginae*
Bloodleaf – *Iresine herbstii*
Blue echeveria – *Echeveria glauca*
Blushing bromeliad – *Neoregelia carolinae* (syn. *Nidularium fulgens*)
Blushing philodendron – *Philodendron erubescens*
Bo-tree – *Ficus religiosa*
Boston fern – *Nephrolepis exaltata* 'Bostoniensis'
Brake fern – *Pteris cretica*
Brazilian tree fern – *Blechnum brasiliense*
Bunny ears – *Opuntia microdasys*
Bush violet – Browallia
Busy Lizzie – Impatiens
Butterfly flower – Schizanthus
Button fern – *Pellaea rotundifolia*
Cabbage tree – *Cordyline australis*
Calamondin orange – × *Citrofortunella microcarpa*
Canary date palm – *Phoenix canariensis*
Canary Island ivy – *Hedera canariensis*
Candle plant – *Plectranthus coleoides* 'Marginatus'
Cape heath – *Erica gracilis, E. hyemalis*

Cape ivy – *Senecio macroglossus*
Cape jasmine – Gardenia
Cape primrose – Streptocarpus
Carrion flower – Stapelia
Carpathian bellflower – *Campanula carpatica*
Cast iron plant – *Aspidistra elatior*
Chandelier plant – *Kalanchoe tubiflora*
Chinese evergreen – Aglaonema
Chinese hibiscus – *Hibiscus rosa-sinensis*
Christmas begonia – Begonia Lorraine-type
Christmas cactus – *Zygocactus truncatus* (syn. *Schlumbergera truncata*)
Christmas cheer – *Sedum rubrotinctum*

Christmas cherry – *Solanum capsicastrum – S. pseudocapsicum*
Christmas pepper – Capsicum
Cineraria – botanically *Senecio cruentus* (syn. S. *hybridus*)
Clog plant – *Hypocyerta glabra*
Coconut palm – *Cocos nucifera*
Common wax plant – Hoya, *Stephanotis floribunda*
Crab cactus – Zygocactus
Creeping Charlie – *Pilea nummularifolia*
Creeping fig – *Ficus pumila*
Croton – Codiaeum
Crown cactus – Rebutia
Crown of thorns – *Euphorbia milii* (syn. E. *splendens*)
Curly palm – *Howea belmoreana* (syn. *Kentia belmoreana*)
Daffodil – Narcissus
Date palm – *Phoenix dactylifera*
Desert fan palm – Washingtonia
Desert privet – *Peperomia obtusifolia*
Devil's backbone – *Kalanchoe daigremontiana* (syn. *Bryophyllum daigremontianum*)
Devil's ivy – *Scindapsus aureus* (syn. *Epipremnum aureum*)
Devil's tongue – *Ferocactus latispinus*
Dinner plate aralia – *Polyscias fruticosa*
Donkey's tail – *Sedum morganianum*
Dragon tree – Dracaena
Dumb cane – Dieffenbachia
Dwarf coconut palm – *Cocos weddeliana*
Earth star – Cryptanthus
Easter cactus – *Rhipsalidopsis gaertneri* (syn. *Schlumbergera gaertneri*)
Elephant's ear – *Philodendron domesticum*
European fan palm – *Chamaerops humilis*
Fairy primrose – *Primula malacoides*
Fairy rose – *Rosa chinensis* 'Minima'

False aralia – *Dizygotheca elegantissima*
False castor oil plant – *Fatsia japonica*
False Jerusalem cherry – *Solanum Capsicastrum*
Fan palm – Chamaerops
Fiddle-leaf fig – *Ficus lyrata*
Fiddle-leaf philodendron – *Philodendron panduriforme*
Fig – Ficus
Finger aralia – *Dizygotheca elegantissima*
Firecracker flower – *Crossandra infundibuliformis*
Fishhook cactus – *Ferocactus latispinus*
Fishtail fern – *Polystichum falcatum*
Fishtail palm – *Caryota mitis*
Flame nettle – Coleus
Flaming Katy – *Kalanchoe blossflediana*
Flaming sword – *Vriesea splendens*
Flamingo flower – Anthurium
Freckle face – *Hypoestes sanguinolenta* (syn. H. *phyllostachya*)
Friendship plant – *Pilea involucrata*
Geranium – Pelargonium
Geranium, scented-leaved – Pelargonium
Germany ivy – *Senecio mikanioides*
Gingham golf ball – *Euphorbia obesa*
Glory bower – *Clerodendrum thomsoniae*
Gloxinia – botanically *Sinningia speciosa*
Gold dust dracaena – *Dracaena godseffiana* (syn. *Dracaena surculosa*)
Golden barrel cactus – *Echinocactus grusonii*
Golden pothos – *Epipremnum aureum*
Golden Tom Thumb cactus – *Parodia aureispina*
Goldfish plant – Columnea
Good Luck Plant – *Cordyline fruticosa*
Goosefoot plant – *Syngonium podophyllum*
Grape ivy – *Cissus rhombifolia* (syn. R. *Rhoicissus rhomboidea*)
Green brake fern – *Pellaea viridis*
Green earth star – *Cryptanthus acaulis*
Hare's foot fern – Davallia
Hearts entangled – *Ceropegia woodii*
Heather – Erica
Hedgehog cactus – *Echinocactus pectinatus*
Holly fern – *Cyrtomium falcatum* (syn. *Polystichum falcatum*)
House lime – *Sparmannia africana*
Hyacinth – Hyacinthus
Inch plant – Tradescantia and Zebrina
Indian azalea – *Rhododendron simsii*
Iron cross begonia – *Begonia masoniana*
Italian bellflower – *Campanula isophylla*
Ivy – *Hedera helix*
Ivy peperomia – *Peperomia griseoargentea*
Ivy tree – x *Fatshedera*
Japanese aralia – *Fatsia japonica*
Ivy-leavved geranium – *Pelargonium peltatum*
Jade tree – *Crassula argentea*
Japanese aralia – *Fatsia japonica*
Japanese azalea – *Rhododendron obtusum*
Jasmine – Jasminum
Jasmine, white – *Jasminum officinale*
Jasmine, pink – *Jasminum polyanthum*
Jelly beans – *Sedum pachyphyllum*
Jerusalem cherry – *Solanum capsicastrum, S. pseudocapsicum*
Joseph's coat – Codiaeum

Glossary

Aerial root A root that grows from the stem above ground level.

Air layering Method of propagating a plant by encouraging a stem to root while still on the plant.

Alkaline compost A growing medium containing lime, and having a high pH.

Annual A plant that lives for one year.

Areole A small depression or raised, cushion-like area on a cactus that bears spines or wool.

Bloom When used to describe the appearance of a leaf or fruit, a whitish or bluish powdery or waxy coating, which is easily removed by rubbing.

Bract A modified leaf, often brightly coloured and petal-like, associated with flowers that themselves lack size or colour. Some bracts are small and scale-like, however, and serve mainly to protect buds.

Bulb Although the term is often used to include corms and tubers, strictly speaking, a bulb is a structure consisting of modified leaves that protects the next season's embryo shoots and flowers.

Bulbil A small bulb that forms above ground. Bulbils can be removed and potted up to grow into bulbs.

Callus A growth of corky tissue that forms over a wound, sealing it.

Cane cuttings Method of propagation using a piece of stem cut into small lengths placed horizontally in the rooting medium.

Cladode *See Cladophyll*

Cladophyll Also called a cladode. A modified stem that simulates a leaf in appearance and function. They can be found in the garden plant *Ruscus aculeatus.*

Compost (potting soil) The medium in which pot plants are grown.

Corm A swollen stem base that usually remains underground and stores food during the dormant season. If cut across, no distinct layers of leaves can be seen, unlike a bulb.

Corolla A term applied to the petals of a flower, or the inner ring of them, the petals being either separate or fused.

Crown The point at which stem and roots meet.

Dormant period The time when growth slows down and the plant needs less warmth and water.

Epiphyte A plant that grows above ground level, usually in trees. Epiphytes are not parasites and only use their host for physical support.

Epiphytic A plant that grows on other plants without being parasitic.

Ericaceous When used specifically the term applies to members of the *Ericaceae* family, but is sometimes applied broadly to include similar plants. If applied to potting soils (potting composts) it means one specially formulated with a low pH.

Eye A term with several meanings. If used with reference to a flower it indicates that the centre of the bloom is a different colour. In propagation it refers to a stem cutting with a single lateral bud. If applied to a tuber, it is used to describe a dormant (undeveloped) bud on its surface.

Eye cuttings Method of propagation using a section of ripened stem with a growth bud, the cutting being placed horizontally in the rooting medium.

Foliar feed A quick-acting liquid fertilizer that can be absorbed through the leaves as well as the roots.

Glochid A tiny barbed spine or bristle, usually occurring in tufts on the areoles of some cacti. These penetrate the skin easily and can often set up irritation, making some cacti hazardous to handle.

Hardy Frost-tolerant.

Hormone, rooting hormone An organic compound that stimulates a fresh young cutting into forming roots.

Humidifier A device for raising the humidity in a room. Sometimes a tray of evaporating water is used, but more sophisticated humidifiers are electrically powered.

Loam-based compost (potting soil) A soil mix in which the main ingredient is sterilized loam, to which peat (peat moss), sand and fertilizer are added.

Mulch A protective covering for soil. Here it refers to a loose covering of chipped bark, peat (peat moss), or similar material used to cover bulbs planted in pots, giving them a period of darkness in preparation for early flowering.

Offset A small plant that is produced alongside its parent.

Peat-based compost (peat-moss-based potting soil) A soil mix in which peat is the main ingredient. Sometimes sand and other substances are added, and the mixture always includes fertilizers and something to neutralize the acidity of the peat.

Perennial A plant that lives for more than two years.

Perlite An inert growing medium, sometimes used as a compost (potting soil) additive or for rooting cuttings.

Petiole A leaf stalk.

pH A scale expressing the degree of acidity or alkalinity of a substance. It runs from 0 to 14, 7 being technically neutral, though most plants prefer a pH of about 6.5. Above 7 is alkaline, below 7 is acid.

Phyllode A leaf stalk that takes on the function and appearance of a leaf. They are commonly found in acacias.

Pinnate A compound leaf with the leaflets arranged in parallel rows.

Prop roots Special roots that arise above ground level and help to give the mature plant stability.

Pseudobulb A thickened, bulb-like stem found on some orchids, used by the plant for water storage, and vary in shape and size. They are always produced above the ground.

Relative humidity The amount of water contained in the air at a particular temperature. It is calculated against the maximum amount of water that could be held in the air at that temperature.

Resting period see Dormant period.

Rhizome A special, modified stem, sometimes thick and fleshy but not always, that lies close to the surface of the soil (except in epiphytes) and produces both roots and aerial parts such as leaves and flowers. You can tell that a rhizome is not a root by the presence of nodes (joints) and often scale-like leaves or buds.

Root-ball A mass of roots and compost (potting soil) together.

Spadix A special type of fleshy flower spike, found in aroids and palms, in which small flowers are more or less embedded. In aroids it is surrounded by a spathe, forming a single erect organ. In palms it is often branched.

Spathe The term usually refers to the conspicuous bract that protects a spadix (see above). In aroids (members of the *Araceae* family, such as philodendrons and monsteras) it is leafy, more or less fleshy, and often brightly coloured. The term is sometimes used for palms (in which it could be fleshy or woody) and other plants – for example, the membranous sheath that surrounds a daffodil bud is technically a spathe. In this book it is always used in the sense described for aroids.

Spores Minute reproductive structure found on non-flowering plants such as ferns and mosses. Can be sown like seeds but need special treatment.

Stem cutting Method of propagation using a length of stem. There are many kinds, including soft, unripened wood, hardwood, and semiripe cuttings, the length varying according to the type of plant.

Stipule A leafy or bract-like appendage at the base of a leaf stalk. It is usually small and inconspicuous.

Sucker A shoot growing from a plant's roots or underground stem, producing leaves of its own. Suckers can be a problem on grafted plants in the garden, but for pot plants they usually provide a useful method of propagation. The term also applies to a group of insects, but is not used in that sense in this publication.

Terrestrial Growing in soil – a land plant.

Tip cutting Method of propagation using only the soft tips of actively growing plants.

Tuber A swollen underground stem or root used by plants to store food during the dormant period.

Vermiculite An inert growing medium, sometimes used as a compost (potting soil) additive or for rooting cuttings.

Viviparous Producing live young. When applied to plants it refers to buds or bulbs that become plantlets while still attached to the parent plant. It also refers to seeds that germinate while on the parent plant.

Whorl Three or more organs, such as leaves, arranged in a circle around the same axis.

NOTES

NOTES

NOTES

NOTES